MARTIN LUTHER KING
COLLECTION ON
NON-VIOLENCE

Presented By
H. Vail Deale

ROOTS of RESISTANCE

Roots *of* RESISTANCE

The Nonviolent Ethic of

MARTIN LUTHER KING, JR.

William D. Watley

Judson Press® Valley Forge

Credits

From *My Life with Martin Luther King, Jr.*, by Coretta Scott King. Copyright © 1969 by Coretta Scott King. Reprinted by permission of Holt, Rinehart and Winston, Publishers.

Roger L. Shinn, excerpt from *Tangled World*. Copyright © 1965 Roger L. Shinn. Reprinted by permission of Charles Scribner's Sons.

Reinhold Niebuhr, excerpted from *Moral Man in an Immoral Society*. Copyright © 1932 Charles Scribner's Sons; copyright renewed © 1960 Reinhold Niebuhr. Reprinted with permission of Charles Scribner's Sons.

Lerone Bennett, Jr., *What Manner of Man: A Biography of Martin Luther King., Jr.* Reprinted by permission of Lerone Bennett, Jr., © 1964 Johnson Publishing Company, Inc.

Specified excerpts passim from *Stride Toward Freedom*, by Martin Luther King, Jr. Copyright © 1958 by Martin Luther King, Jr. Reprinted by permission of Harper and Row, Publishers, Inc.

Specified excerpts passim from *The Trumpet of Conscience*, by Martin Luther King, Jr. Copyright © 1967 by Martin Luther King, Jr. Reprinted by permission of Harper and Row, Publishers, Inc.

Specified excerpts passim from *Why We Can't Wait*, by Martin Luther King, Jr. Copyright © 1964 by Martin Luther King, Jr. Reprinted by permission of Harper and Row, Publishers, Inc.

Specified excerpts passim from *Where Do We Go from Here?: Chaos or Community*, by Martin Luther King, Jr. Copyright © 1967 by Martin Luther King, Jr. Reprinted by permission of Harper and Row, Publishers, Inc.

Martin Luther King, Jr., *Strength to Love*. Reprinted by permission of Joan Daves. Copyright © 1963 by Martin Luther King, Jr.

Martin Luther King, Jr., "A Comparison of the Conception of God in the Thinking of Paul Tillich and Henry Nelson Wieman" (Ph.D. dissertation, Boston University, 1955). Reprinted by permission of Joan Daves. Copyright © 1977 by the Estate of Martin Luther King, Jr.

Martin Luther King, Jr., "What a Christian Should Believe About Himself," from the King Papers, 1955-1961. Reprinted by permission of Joan Daves. Copyright © Martin Luther King, Jr., and the Estate of Martin Luther King, Jr.

Library of Congress Cataloging-in-Publication Data
Watley, William D.
  Roots of resistance.

  Bibliography: p.
  Includes index.
  1. King, Martin Luther—Views on nonviolence.
  2. Nonviolence.   3. Afro-Americans—Biography.
  4. Baptists—United States—Clergy—Biography.
  I. Title.
E185.97.K5W33   1985   323.4'092'4   85-24176
ISBN 0-8170-1092-0

Acknowledgments

This book is the culmination of a long study process which has been both formal and informal. This process has lasted on and off for fourteen of the seventeen years of my marriage. For the greater part of my marriage, my wife, Muriel, has had to put up with my preoccupation, late nights of reading, long periods of writing and reflection, and innumerable conversations about Martin King. Not once has she complained. I am pleased, therefore, to dedicate this book to her.

I am indebted to Dr. Roger Shinn, of Union Theological Seminary of New York City, who was my major professor during my tenure there and who has remained a strong supporter through the years. He encouraged me to publish long before I had given much thought to doing so.

I continue to be grateful to my sister and friend, beloved Carolyn Scavella, who served as the first reader and editor for this manuscript, as well as for my previous publication *Sermons from the Black Pulpit*. For her, as well as for her husband and my friend, Donald, whose patience, understanding, and support made Carolyn's editorial job easier when she and I debated often, long, and at times late, I am indeed thankful.

I am also indebted to my administrative assistant, Mrs. Marie Russell, for painstakingly typing this manuscript with the willing spirit and Christian character for which she is so well known.

I thank Judson Press for its commitment to the Christian ideals that Dr. King embodied and for its work with me in refining this manuscript.

Foreword

Among the mysteries of history is the appearance from time to time of leaders who defy all laws of probability. In the language of the Old Testament, God in times of human need sometimes "raises up" a prophet, a judge, a deliverer, a priest, or a shepherd. Today we think up intricate schemes of economic, social, and psychological causation to account for the emergence of unexpected leaders, but we do not do much better, and often we do worse, than the simpler language of the Bible.

So it was with the rise of Martin Luther King, Jr. Before the fact, who would have predicted that one of the great social leaders of this century—a Nobel Laureate in peace, the inspiration for a national holiday in the United States—would be a black Baptist preacher? But that is what happened.

I was in the presence of King only three times—and what a presence it was! I saw him enter into conversation, devise strategies, respond to critical questions, and move people to act on their highest loyalties. On many more occasions I watched him on television, demonstrating courage and compassion under stress. I read most of his published writings and much of the literature about him. Yet I would not dare to explain him or claim to understand him.

Far more often I have talked with William Watley about King. Together we have searched, he leading the way, for the secrets of King's leadership. And we have tried to define with some precision the qualities of King's belief and practice in nonviolent methods of social change. We, too, want to change society, and we ask what is possible and what is ethical in bringing about change.

Two themes stand out in Dr. Watley's book about Dr. King. One is his deep understanding of King's roots in the black church. Watley shows these in ways that I, without his guidance, would not be able to recognize or appreciate. The other is his careful investigation of King's belief in and practice of nonviolence. Watley looks into King's writings and actions with an admiration that does not dim criticism and a criticism that does not destroy admiration.

Of all King's words, I suppose the most famous are "I have a dream." Yet in addition to being a visionary, King was also a strategist and tactician. The issue was always how to relate the dream and the tactics. How does any believer combine constancy of conviction—in King's case, conviction about love and justice, which are ingrained in human nature and in the universe—with innovative tactics that respond to ever-changing situations?

Watley shows us that King's tactics were not simply the applications of principles worked out in advance. King did not plan and prepare for his career of leadership. His role was thrust upon him. He had to grope, experiment, seek allies, maneuver against opponents, negotiate, build on victories, and respond to frustrations and defeats. Watley skillfully combines the narrative of King's public encounters with the analysis of his use of power in his successive campaigns.

King believed, as Watley shows, that love and justice often require conflict. Committed to nonviolence, he sought to "negotiate from strength"—a phrase that in our time is often used in ways totally opposed to King's. One of King's phrases was "constructive coercive power," employed to disclose or create tension that could lead to reconciliation. So Watley suggests that King's tactics could be "coercive" and "manipulative," that his greatest successes came when his opponents were provoked to violence, that the threat of violence by his followers and allies was a factor in his nonviolent campaigns and negotiations.

Watley himself comes out a little closer than King to those Latin American theologians of liberation who, without glorifying violence, see so much violence imbedded in society that they believe that Christians cannot totally detach themselves from that violence. Yet he recognizes that King, by appealing to the conscience of the society while exerting pressure, achieved what coercive power alone could not accomplish.

It is a virtue of this book that the writer does not end by prescribing all the answers. He is able to say that King's ethic was at times "simplistic"—and to say this without condescension and without claiming to define an entirely adequate ethic. One of the messages of the book is that any serious faith— certainly any Christian faith—requires resolute commitments, but ethical activity is not the whole of faith. This message is consistent with the claim, here made so persuasively, that Martin Luther King, Jr., was above all a black Christian preacher.

Roger L. Shinn
Union Theological Seminary
New York, New York

Contents

Introduction

Finally, be strong in the Lord and in the strength of his might. Put on the whole armor of God, that you may be able to stand against the wiles of the devil. For we are not contending against flesh and blood, but against the principalities, against the powers, against the world rulers of this present darkness, against the spiritual hosts of wickedness in the heavenly places" (Ephesians 6:10-12).

The writer of Ephesians states that the Christian's struggle in the world is essentially systemic. The greatest adversaries to human freedom are not other people but structures of evil which are present in the world. The "principalities" and "powers" "are two of the orders of spirits (angels or demons) which, in the astrological thinking of the time, were held to have a dominion over human life."[1] The essence of Christian warfare is found in resisting the demonic forces or systems or orders of evil that dehumanize, oppress, and prevent persons from achieving that full humanity which, Christians believe, God wills for them and which the blood of Christ makes possible. John Yoder has stated it in another way: "The believer strives ultimately not against tangible men and objects ('flesh and blood,' verse 12), but against the Powers they obey."[2] How one responds to the dehumanizing and demonic presence in the world, with its systemic violence and multifarious sins, is a question that has perplexed every Christian who is socially and politically conscious.

While the issue of Christian prophetic witness in a world of institutionalized evil is as old as the Christian faith itself, it is also as current as any news story in which Christians, in the attempt to act out the implications of their faith, find themselves in conflict with either the state itself or its laws, institutions, or policies. It is more than the question of moral versus civil disobedience. It is essentially the ethical concern of Christian responsibility in a world of ethical relativities.

The matter of Christian prophetic witness in a world dominated by the principalities and powers (political, social, and economic) raises a number of questions. First, what is the relationship between faith and politics, between moral absolutes and an ethical system based on pragmatics? Second, "How can Christians, children of God's love and followers of Jesus Christ, live and work in a world where the use of force and violence against the countless forms of human sin (such as political oppression, racism, and economic exploitation) seems unavoidable?"[3]

Third, how can one engage in dialogue with a party who not only does not speak the same language but who also operates from an entirely different set of assumptions and whose perspective of the world and the meaning of life consequently differs? Further, if one's basic posture is not essentially moralistic, but is legalistic, political, or economic, the question of morality becomes passé, and the attempts to appeal to conscience and to arouse guilt feelings become inconsequential. Fourth, how does one either convert or defeat an opponent who cannot be personalized? How does one defend oneself against and "outstrategize" foes such as institutional racism and economic exploitation, the co-conspirators of the systemic effort to thwart the aspirations of oppressed minorities?

This book is the story of one man's struggles to come to grips with these and other related questions concerning how a Christian engages the principalities and powers. This book is the story of the development and application of the nonviolent ethic of Martin Luther King, Jr. King agreed with the perspective of the writer of Ephesians concerning the nature of prophetic Christian witness in the world.

He saw himself "contending against the principalities" in that he lifted the focus of the civil rights movement from a personal level to an ideological one. He considered whites as well as blacks to be subjected equally to the principalities and powers because he considered both blacks and whites to be victims in an evil system of institutionalized racism. According to Herbert Richardson:

> King's perception of the human problem today as rooted in a certain structure of social evil led him to emphasize again and again that his struggle was directed against the forces, or structure, or evil itself rather than against the person or group who is doing the evil. Christian faith sees neither particular men nor particular groups as evil, but sees them trapped within a structure of ideological separation which makes ritual conflict inevitable.[4]

Nonviolence for King was more than a strategy or a methodology for addressing racial issues; it was a personal and social ethic. King's basic theological and ethical perspective was founded on the bedrock of black religion and then shaped by his formal theological education. Much of his thought, however, particularly regarding nonviolence, was refined and, at times, reshaped in the midst of conflict and action. King's nonviolent ethic was an "ethic of exigencies" in that it was honed in the midst of those crisis situations and developed through the conflict engendered by black protest against the institutional and personal racism of white America. In addition to the Montgomery bus boycott, some of the other Southern campaigns such as Albany, Birmingham, and Selma, which helped to develop King's nonviolent ethic, are examined. Toward the end of his life King primarily addressed himself to the issues of economic justice and international peace. These aspects of King's maturing ethic, or ethic in transition, represented by the Chicago campaign and his opposition to the Vietnam war, are discussed. The philosophical or theoretical components, or principles, of King's nonviolent ethic are also discussed.

One of the questions that this book will focus upon is what do King's ethics and methods mean for socially sensitive persons, such as Christians, trying to resist violence, inequality, and injustice today?

1

Formative Influences: Black Religious Experience, Evangelical Liberalism, Personalism

Throughout the brief span of his life and ministry Martin Luther King, Jr., remained the product of the black religious experience. There is no understanding of Martin Luther King, Jr., without an understanding of black religion. This statement may be more radical and have more profound implications for understanding King as a nonviolent theorist and practitioner than may be obvious at first glance.

The black church has been acknowledged as the social and political base for the civil rights movement which King led. The influence of black religion upon King as a homiletician or orator is undeniable. At his core, King was neither philosopher nor academician nor organizational administrator. He was essentially a black preacher. To be more precise, he was essentially a black pastor. Although history has carved a much greater role for him and although he felt himself to be called or caught or trapped by the *zeitgeist*, King's basic call was that of shepherd to the flock of Christ. The point is that black religion was the basis for King's preaching style; the black church was the organizational context for the movement which made, and which was made by, King; and both the black religion and the black church were the central influences in shaping King's theological posture. Martin King has been classified theologically as an evangelical liberal. In the initial stages of his development as a theologue, King's self- and vocational understanding were nurtured by the broadening exposure and experience at the predominantly black institution of higher learning, Morehouse College in his native Atlanta, Georgia. One of the great untold stories of King's life is the significance of Morehouse College for his personal and intellectual development. It was during his Morehouse years that King decided upon the Christian ministry as a vocation. When he first entered college, King was considering a career in either medicine or law. He had thought about the ministry but had been repelled by what he considered at that time to be the "emotionalism" that was characteristic of much of the black Christian worship tradition and the lack of formal education among a majority of the black clergy. While at Morehouse, however, King came under the influence of Dr. Benjamin Mays, the college president; Dr. George Kelsey, chairperson of the religion department; and Dr. Samuel Williams, professor of philosophy. These formally trained ministers, whose teaching and preaching had theological and hermeneutic depth as well as a social and prophetic dimension, changed King's perception of the ministry as a vocation. During his junior year King told his parents of his decision to enter the ministry. Much has been written about the influence upon Martin King of George W. Davis of Crozer Seminary and Edgar Sheffield Brightman and L. Harold DeWolf of Boston University Divinity School. However, such men as Benjamin Mays, George Kelsey, and Samuel Williams, as well as others at Morehouse College, were the intellectual fathers and spiritual mentors for King. These black intellectual giants of Morehouse laid the foundation for King's later work at Crozer Seminary and Boston University in the same way that black religion and the black church laid the foundation for his appropriation of evangelical liberalism and personalism. Crozer Theological Seminary, at the time King attended, was regarded as liberal in its theological orientation. While there King was influenced by Dr. George Washington Davis, professor of Christian theology at the seminary and a leading evangelical liberal among the faculty members at Crozer. Dr. Davis seemed to have impressed King more than did his other professors. King described Davis as "a marvelous teacher conversant with the trends of modern culture and yet sincerely religious. He was warm and Christian. It was easy to get close to him."[1] Out of the one hundred and ten hours required for graduation from Crozer, King took thirty-four of them with Davis.[2] It was Professor Davis who helped King make the transition from fundamentalism to that branch of liberalism known as "evangelical."

Although several schools of liberal thought were represented on the Crozer faculty, the major division was between the "evangelicals" and the "moderns." The evangelical liberals were those serious Christians who sought to develop a theology acceptable to intelligent moderns. "They stood squarely within the Christian tradition and accepted as normative for their thinking what they understood to be the essence of historical Christianity."[3] The modernistic liberals, on the other hand, were those "intelligent moderns who still wanted to be regarded as serious Christians."[4] They believed there were elements in the Christian tradition which ought to be retained. However, the standard by which the abiding values of historical Christianity were to be measured was derived from the presupposition of modern science, philosophy, psychology, and social thought.[5] Dr. Davis epitomized evangelical liberalism at its best. At Crozer, he helped many students, including Martin King, avoid the extremes of fundamentalism on the one hand and humanism on the other. Some students in their revolt against fundamentalism went to the other end of the theological spectrum. King never did. "It was the kind of liberalism represented by George W. Davis which made the difference."[6]

In order to understand the impact that the liberalism represented by Dr. Davis had upon the developing ethical consciousness of Martin King, we should examine the major themes of Davis's liberal theology.[7] A number of them are consistent with the beliefs which are affirmed and proclaimed in traditional black preaching as well as practiced in traditional black church life. Evangelical liberalism was a refining process rather than the primary source for thoughts which were already present in King's mind—thoughts that had been implanted there by the teachings inherent in black religion and the black church. Evangelical liberalism provided the label for a container whose ingredients were already present in King. King's receptivity to evangelical liberalism and his openness to the instruction of George Washington Davis were based to a great extent on the congruence between these ideas and the beliefs that King brought with him to Crozer from his background in the black church.

A Moral Order in the Universe

One of the themes of the liberalism espoused by George W. Davis was the belief in the existence of a moral order in the universe. Just as there are laws of the empirical sciences which govern and support the physical processes of the universe, so, too, there are moral laws which determine its inner life and character. The order of the universe, then, is more than a matter of physics; it is a theological affirmation as well. God is a moral God; human life has meaning; and history has a goal. Thus, the character and inner life of the universe govern and support the goal of history and the meaning of human existence which have been determined by a moral God. Davis once wrote:

> To be sure, the struggle to stand where one is obedient to the voice of conscience, of moral law, or of God has never been an easy one. . . . There is a certain "logic of events" in history, a certain definiteness of purpose and intention running through the pageant of the centuries, to which the wise man will not close his eyes.[8]

Martin King also believed in the existence of a moral order. He believed in moral absolutes and rejected any system of theological relativities. He decried any ethic whose principles or standards were either governed by the logic of the situation or were determined by majority consensus. In the sermon "A Knock at Midnight" King talked about a moral midnight:

> It is also midnight within the moral order. At midnight colors lose their distinctiveness and become a sullen shade of gray. Moral principles have lost their distinctiveness. For modern man, absolute right and absolute wrong is a matter of what the majority is doing. Right and wrong are relative to likes and dislikes and customs of a particular community. We have unconsciously applied Einstein's theory of relativity, which properly described the physical universe, to the moral and ethical realm.[9]

King, however, also went on to express his faith in the ultimate triumph of the moral order. One of his favorite statements was "the arc of moral universe may be long, but it bends toward justice." He would often quote William Cullen Bryant's statement: "Truth, crushed to earth, shall rise again" and Thomas Carlyle's affirmation: "No lie you can speak or act but it will come, after longer or shorter circulation, like a bill drawn on Nature's Reality, and be presented there for a payment,—with the answer, No effects."[10] In the sermon "Our God Is Able" he said:

> These great changes are not mere political and sociological shifts.
> . . . They represent the inevitable decay of any system based on principles that are not in harmony with the moral laws of the universe. . . . [God] has placed within the very structure of this universe certain absolute moral laws. We can neither defy them nor break them. If we disobey them, they will break us. The forces of evil may temporarily conquer truth, but truth will ultimately conquer its conqueror. Our God is able.[11]

King, as did Davis, affirmed the existence of the moral order and expressed faith in its ultimate triumph. Down through the years, in sermon and song, in Sunday school lessons and Bible studies, black religion has expressed its belief in the existence of a moral order. Black people have maintained this belief in the face of what some would regard as incontrovertible historic evidence to the contrary. This belief has been asserted despite centuries of dehumanizing slavery and over a century of psychologically debilitating Jim Crowism. This belief has been affirmed despite a continuing legacy of institutional and personal, economic and legal, and cultural and social racism. Blacks have refused to accept either the proposition that there is no ultimate purpose or meaning for their lives or that ultimate meaning is found in their being hewers of wood and drawers of water.

The issue of theodicy has always been and, as long as racism and injustice exist, will continue to be one of the central concerns of black theological reflection. However, the belief that there is a moral order to the universe, or that one reaps what one sows, is one of the more prevalent themes in traditional black preaching and one that King believed.

When one looks at the harsh historical contradictions and brutalizing existential situations that black folk have endured and continue to endure, one realizes that their insistence upon a moral order is just short of miraculous. This openness to a moral universe within the black psyche may possibly reach as far back as black antiquity in Africa. Whites may have introduced blacks to Christianity—and done so from a twisted perspective—but they did not introduce blacks to God and to the practice of religion. Black people had their own theological perspectives before American slavery. Much of that perspective revolved around the cyclical processes of nature and, thus, bespoke an orderliness to life and the universe. The traditional African mindset did not make the Western distinction between the sacred and the profane. Rather, life was viewed as all of one piece, and the moral order was inextricably interwoven with the physical universe. Within the black religious psyche or perspective, then, a concept of moral order or of orderliness operating within the universe has existed since African antiquity.

Because of the many assaults upon the personhood of black people, a moral order which gave ultimate purpose to life was a necessary theological corrective to historical reality. Because so much of life and history did not make sense, black people needed to know about and affirm a moral order beyond the historical setting. This order gave meaning to their personhood and lives as they functioned within the historical setting. It gave hope that there would be justice in the future. Because of the large degree of insecurity and relativity of their lives, particularly when the application of legal statutes to their cases and on their behalf was involved, black people needed to know that there were moral absolutes and principles in the universe. These principles could not be shaken and were immune to the politics of jurisprudence, the biases of educational institutions, the oppression inherent within bourgeois capitalism, and the historic discrimination of white culture and society. Black preachers, many of whom functioned without formal theological education, understood not only the needs of their people but also the message of the Scriptures. Through the Scriptures they spoke forcefully to the needs of the people.

The black religious perspective not only embodied a belief in the existence of a moral order, but also expressed faith in its ultimate triumph. Even in slavery, as can be seen in the biblical hermeneutics expressed in the spirituals, black people articulated their belief in the triumph of good over evil, right over wrong, and justice over injustice. Take the words of songs such as the following:

> Didn't my Lord deliver Daniel,
> deliver Daniel, deliver Daniel,
> Didn't my Lord deliver Daniel
> An' why not a every man.

> He delivered Daniel from de lion's den,
> Jonah f'om de belly of de whale,
> an' de Hebrew chillun f'om de fiery furnace,
> an' why not a every man.

And

> O Mary, don't you weep, don't you mourn,
> O Mary, don't you weep, don't you mourn;
> Pharaoh's army got drownded,
> O Mary, don't you weep.

And

> Joshua fit de battle ob Jerico, Jerico, Jerico,
> Joshua fit de battle ob Jerico,
> An' de walls come tumblin' down.

These are words of faith in the triumph of justice.

Blacks have always affirmed belief in a brighter day ahead. That brighter day has been placed sometimes within the historical framework and at other times within the eschatological dimension. Much has been written about the pie-in-the-sky character of black preaching, or the opiate effect of black religion upon the social and political consciousness of black people. One cannot deny that religion has functioned as escapism for blacks, as it has functioned in the same way for whites (both poor and middle-class whites). However, it is also true that the belief in the triumph of the moral order has inspired blacks to work for justice and sacrifice their very lives for change within the historic realm. Such a belief has helped generations of black parents not only endure abuse, but also make untold sacrifices for the education and well-being of their children. It has encouraged many young black persons with a vision of fulfilling their God-given potential to fight against all kinds of crippling odds to become "somebody."

Consequently, the belief in a moral order and its triumph

espoused by the evangelical liberalism of George W. Davis was not new for the young Martin King. That perspective had been part of King's own religious heritage. He heard that perspective expressed in black pulpits and saw the hope which it represented at work in the praxis of the black church.

God Works in History

Another major theme found in the liberalism represented by George W. Davis, which was closely related to the belief in the moral order, was the belief that God works in history. Davis wrote:

> God and history belong together. He who separates them loses one of our best sources for the empirical observation of God's ways and his purpose with man. The key to history is lost when God is separated from the stream of events. And this, for the simple reason that, while history shows man in action, it also discloses to open mind and sensitive heart the unwearied action of the living God, yet toiling to establish his kingdom over all the earth. [12]

King also believed that God works in history. For example, King cited Montgomery, Alabama, as God's deliberate historical choice for the beginning of the latter-day thrust by black people for full equality. In *Stride Toward Freedom* King stated:

> There is a creative power that works to pull down mountains of evil and level hilltops of injustice. God still works through history His wonders to perform. It seems as though God had decided to use Montgomery as the proving ground for the struggle and triumph of freedom and justice in America. And what better place for it than the leading symbol of the Old South? It is one of the splendid ironies of our day that Montgomery, the Cradle of the Confederacy, is being transformed into Montgomery, the cradle of freedom and justice. [13]

Not only in Montgomery but also in every nonviolent campaign that he waged throughout his life, King expressed his belief that God was involved in the historic moment. Prayer was as much a part of a King-led campaign as were the strategy sessions. Many of the decisions that were made regarding the specifics of a campaign were reached only after King had prayed about them. He believed that God was with him, guiding and supporting the struggle and strengthening those who were suffering for the righteous cause of freedom. In *Strength to Love* he wrote:

> Above all, we must be reminded anew that God is at work in his universe. He is not outside the world looking on with a sort of cold indifference. Here on all the roads of life, he is striving in our striving. Like an ever-loving Father, he is working through history for the salvation of his children. As we struggle to defeat the forces of evil, the God of the universe struggles with us.[14]

King often used the traditional biblical language of the Exodus story to describe the struggle of black people to be free. The towering figure of Moses as leader, Egypt as the condition of oppression, Pharaoh as oppressor, the Red Sea as an obstacle to freedom, the wilderness as the transition period between slavery and freedom, and the Promised Land as freedom are all paradigms for those who were themselves engaged in a similar struggle. The Exodus drama was tailor-made for those like King who believed that God was not just involved in the historical; God was actually directing the events of history. The sermon "The Death of Evil upon the Seashore" was simply one instance when King compared black people's quest for freedom with the Exodus of the Hebrews from Egypt. King, in this sermon, stated:

> Looking back, we see the forces of segregation gradually dying on the seashore. The problem is far from solved and gigantic mountains of opposition lie ahead, but at least we have left Egypt, and with patient yet firm determination we shall reach the Promised Land. Evil in the form of injustice and exploitation shall not survive forever. A Red Sea passage in history ultimately brings the forces of goodness to victory, and the closing of the same water marks the doom and destruction of the forces of evil.[15]

Of course, a casual review of spirituals and early black sermons reveals, as a number of scholars have already shown, that the imagery of the Exodus has always been significant for the black religious imagination. The importance of the Exodus for those early sources of black American religious thought demonstrates that a number of black spirituals, sermons, and prayers were apocalyptic in nature. Apocalyptic literature is the religious expression of a people who are enduring oppression or undergoing persecution. The language is veiled and cryptic, and the major personalities and events of the literature belong to another place and time. However, the intention is to give encouragement to those involved in their own struggle against injustice. Apocalyptic literature offers a paradigm of contemporary situations which provide hope. It does not simply chronicle the machinations of evil but gives the believer the assurance that his or her struggles are not in vain.

Although much of traditional black religious language has been cloaked in biblical language and refers to personalities and events in another place and time, the application has to be made to one's own struggles within history. Deliverance and freedom have a historic context as well as an eschatological dimension. Frederick Douglass stated that some were thinking about heaven when they sang of Canaan and the Promised Land, but to him and some of his companions, those terms meant the North and Canada. Harriet Tubman was called "Moses" because of the number of slaves she led to freedom from the South. She would use the song "Steal Away" as a signal to those who were to journey with her to prepare to travel. The point is that there is within the black religious experience a long tradition of conceptualizing God as being involved not only in the historical process in general, but more specifically in the liberation struggles of black people. This tradition of interpretation goes back to the earliest periods of a developing black hermeneutic. The theme of evangelical liberalism vis-à-vis God's involvement in history was also one which was present in King's own religious heritage and one with which he was well acquainted.

The Essential Social Character of Human Life

Another theme of the liberalism adhered to by Davis was the belief that human existence is essentially social in character. He viewed solidarity as the goal toward which history is moving and human personality as standing a better chance of being realized in society than in isolation, separation, or estrangement from community. Davis saw one of the major shifts of history as being from the individual to the social. He wrote:

> Although we live "in one of the most absolutistic and autocratic ages in all human history," yet, viewed in the large, the trend of life has been away from the right of the individual to dominate and control other people for his selfish advantage. We have been moving toward the solidarity—even the sanctity—of the social group.[16]

Davis did not believe that this shift negated the personal. He believed that personal life had a better chance of being realized in a society which supported and protected the individual than in one where the individual could exploit other persons at will. Davis felt that the goal of life was "individuality *within* fellowship; never is it individualism *against* fellowship. No man, that is to say, has an ultimate right to achieve 'success' at the expense of personal values either in himself or in others."[17]

Martin Luther King affirmed the social character of existence. He rejected segregation because he believed it destroyed community and made "brotherhood" impossible. He believed that all of life is interrelated and that all persons are caught "in an inescapable network of mutuality, tied in a single garment of destiny. Whatever affects one directly, affects all indirectly."[18] It is in life's social dimension that individuality is achieved and personhood is realized. King often asserted, "I can never be what I ought to be until you are what you ought to be, and you can never be what you ought to be until I am what I ought to be. This is the interrelated structure of reality."[19] Although this statement later appears in *Strength to Love* and *The Trumpet of Conscience* and was incorporated in several speeches, it was while Martin King was a student that he wrote:

> The destiny of each individual, wherever he resides on the earth, is tied up with the destiny of all men that inhabit the globe. We literally cannot live entirely to ourselves. When we rise and go to the bath, a cake of soap is handed to us by a Frenchman, or a sponge is handed to us by a Pacific Islander, a towel by a Turk, our underclothes by an American or Englishman. We go down to our breakfast, our tea is poured out by a Chinese. Our toast we accept at the hands of an English-speaking farmer, not to mention the baker. We are indebted to half of the world before we finish breakfast.[20]

Before his death he reaffirmed the belief that had matured and grown to full bloom as his ethical consciousness had developed: "Now the judgment of God is upon us, and we must either learn to live as brothers or we are all going to perish together as fools."[21]

Martin King understood the social character of existence in a deeply personal way. Neither being the son of an influential black Baptist preacher who pastored a sizable and influential congregation in Atlanta, Georgia, nor having a family who was firmly entrenched in Atlanta's solid, black middle-class community bestowed any immunity from racism upon King. King's first encounter with racism occurred during his early childhood. When he was very small, he had two white playmates whose parents owned a small neighborhood store. However, by the time he was of elementary school age, the parents of his white playmates had forbidden them to associate with either King or his brother. It was his mother who responded to Martin's bewilderment in the face of this direct racial rebuff by saying, "Don't let this thing impress you. Don't let it make you feel you're not as good as white people. You're as good as anyone else, and don't you forget it."[22]

As a young black growing up in the South, King encountered racism as it manifested itself on a daily basis. He saw the inhumane and unjust treatment that victims of racism received at the hands of racists. He passed spots where blacks had been lynched, and he witnessed the Ku Klux Klan on its night rides. With his own eyes he witnessed blacks brutalized physically by the police and then mistreated legally in the courts.

King also had more personal experiences with racism, which played a critical role in shaping his personality. An incident which stood out in his mind occurred during his teens when he and other high school students, along with their teacher, were returning by bus from an oratorical contest in Valdosta, Georgia. Upon boarding the bus, the students took the first seats they could find. When the driver asked them to move, they refused until their teacher suggested they do so. The driver, angered because of their initial refusal to move, flew into a rage and cursed King and the others. The students, saying nothing, endured the verbal abuse. King later recalled: "It was a night I'll never forget. I don't think I have ever been so deeply angry in all my life."[23]

In the summer of 1944, King and some other high school students went north to the Hartford, Connecticut, area to work on a tobacco farm. The absence of Jim Crow regulations gave King a sense of freedom that he had never experienced before. Returning to the South at the end of the summer was for him a bitter pill. When he was required to sit behind a curtain in the dining car on his return trip home, King felt as if a curtain had been dropped on his selfhood. This trip to the North intensified King's abhorrence of the Southern system of segregation and, along with some other personal experiences, helped sensitize him to the economic injustice that often accompanies racial prejudice. Although King came from an economically secure and comfortable home, he never forgot the deprivation of some of his playmates and others living around him. In addition, his work experiences in the North made him aware that poor whites are subjected to the same economic exploitation as poor blacks. Thus, even before attending Crozer Seminary, King had a dawning awareness of the social character of existence, particularly regarding racial and economic justice.

As a young black person, King discovered that racism reaches across economic and educational disparities and all other barriers of class consciousness among blacks. Many black persons have made the startling and often painful discovery that one's blackness is the predominating factor of identification in America. (As an aside, and to underscore this point, let us look at an incident in the life of another black social prophet, Malcolm X. In his autobiography, Malcolm X records a time when he was speaking at a white university and his position was being challenged and attacked by a black associate professor, who accused him of being a "divisive demagogue" and a "reverse racist." Malcolm X asked him, "Do you know what white racists call a black Ph.D.?" When the individual answered in the negative, Malcolm X looked at him and said, "Nigger!")[24] No matter how much money one has amassed, or education one has acquired, or prominence one has earned, in a number of places in this society if a face is of ebon hue, the individual is always a "nigger."

The all-pervasive character of racism, then, brings together in black congregational life a unique blend of persons from various walks of life who share not only the same ethnicity, history, and culture, but also a common oppression by racism. It is not unusual in the black church to find "the Ph.D's and no D's" sitting on the same church boards and exercising the same power. (Actually in the black church in a number of instances the latter exercise much more power than the former.) Both have encountered racism in their lives. Both know the pain and the conflict that racism produces. Both battle, on a daily basis, the assaults of racism upon their personhood. Both know the feelings of resentment and sometimes hatred, both of self and sometimes of others, which must be wrestled with and struggled through. These feelings must be dealt with to keep the victim from developing a perception of self, others, and life which is just as warped and twisted as that held by the racist.

Both educated and undereducated blacks know of the theological questions and issues of faith which racism poses for them as victims. Both have had to agonize with their faith and their God concerning these questions. They may live in different neighborhoods, work in different worlds, and enjoy different lifestyles, but on Sunday morning they meet around one common mercy seat. They are blended together by the triune God into one community of faith to share the same cultural experience of divine worship. They are responsive to the same liturgy, are touched by the same music; and both await to see if there is any word from the Lord. They await a word which will make sense out of the perplexities experienced during the last week and a word which will help prepare them for the onslaught of the insidious racism that the coming week has in store.

One recognizes that the cultural dimension of worship can bring together into congregational life groups and persons of like background and experience. The point, however, is that blacks are brought together not simply because of a common culture but also because of a common cross known as racism. Blacks are brought together because of a common heritage and a continuing train of abuse. As a young person growing up in the South, King learned of the social character of existence not only by what he experienced outside of the black church but also by what he experienced and witnessed within the black church.

The black church was a caring and healing community for those who were bound together by a common faith and a common suffering. When one member of the community encountered misfortune, the rest of the community rallied to that member's aid. It was not, and still is not, unusual to see in the church blacks who have had sharp differences of opinion and severe personality conflicts rally to one another's defense in the face of a common enemy. For underneath the infighting and internal politics that take place in the black church is the unarticulated awareness that all blacks are vulnerable at some point. Therefore, if the community of faith does not care for, guide, protect, support, and encourage its own, then no one else will do so.

The liberalism of George W. Davis, along with King's own experiences of witnessing the victimization of poor whites by the same unjust racial and economic system, helped him refine and expand his awareness of the social character of existence. However, the black church, which constituted so much of King's own personal world before he went to Crozer, was also a major factor in his appropriation of this theme into his theological and ethical perspective.

Personalism

Still another major theme espoused by that branch of liberalism taught by George Davis was personalism. Although King later studied under two great personalist figures, Edgar Sheffield Brightman and L. Harold DeWolf, at Boston University, it was George Davis at Crozer who first introduced King to Brightman's personalism. Davis felt that God's intent in history was to produce free personalities. Freedom for Davis did not mean irresponsibility; it involved doing God's will, which is inherent in human nature, since human beings are made in the image of God. Davis felt that the great contribution of Jesus lay in the value and worth that He ascribed to human personality. This, for Davis, meant that the essence of human life is the personal dimension. By the personal dimension, Davis did not mean individualism but rather "that potential quality of life which separates *homo sapiens* from all other forms of creation and, indeed, lifts him above them."[25]

There is a qualitative difference between human beings and all other forms of animal life. Because of this qualitative difference, a human being must always be treated infinitely better than other forms of life. "What he is may have commercial and objective value to the merchant, the farmer, or the slave master;" wrote Davis, "but [man] is also inherently valuable and hence must never be used with the callousness with which one might use a hoe, a truck, a lawn mower, a book, or a carpetbeater."[26] It is because of the inherent value of human beings that persons must always be viewed as ends in themselves and never as means to an end. Davis quoted Immanuel Kant on this point: "So act as to treat humanity, whether in thine own person or in that of any other, in every case as an end withal, never as a means only."[27]

In September 1951 Martin Luther King entered the School of Theology at Boston University to begin work on his doctoral degree in systematic theology. At Boston the two professors who had the greatest impact on King were Edgar Sheffield Brightman, whom he had studied at Crozer with George W. Davis and whose philosophy of personalism was the single most important philosophical influence on Davis's theology, and L. Harold DeWolf, who was King's major professor and adviser for his dissertation. In describing their influence upon his philosophical development, King wrote:

> Both men greatly stimulated my thinking. It was mainly under these teachers that I studied personalistic philosophy—the theory that the clue to the meaning of ultimate reality is found in personality. This personal idealism remains today my basic philosophical conviction.[28]

Personalism had a deep and abiding effect upon King and became the philosophical axis around which a number of his theological and ethical positions revolved. Although he seldom specifically mentioned personalism per se outside of *Stride Toward Freedom*, the influence of personalism, like that of his black religious heritage, is intuitively felt and comes through in a number of ways in King's writings and thought.

For example, as Smith and Zepp have observed,

> It is highly likely that one of the major tenets of King's conception of nonviolence, "the redemptive value of unmerited suffering," was indebted to Brightman in whose thought "the spiritual value of sacrifice and suffering" was one of the essentials of Christian theology.[29]

Such personalistic motifs as the inherent worth of personality, the existence of a moral order, and the social character of human existence were incorporated and became permanent fixtures in King's matured ethical consciousness.

Personalism's conviction that the clue to the meaning of ultimate reality is found in personality became the basis for two of King's fundamental convictions. First, it gave him a metaphysical and a philosophical framework for the idea of a personal God. Second, it gave him a metaphysical base for affirming the dignity and worth of all human personality. The affirmation of the inherent dignity of personality became one of the reasons for King's rejection of segregation. King would often paraphrase the Jewish philosopher Martin Buber and say that segregation "substitutes an 'I-it' relationship for the 'I-thou' relationship, and relegates persons to the status of things. It scars the soul and degrades the personality."[30] In part, King's belief that human beings are ends in themselves caused him to reject communism. He believed that communism made human beings means for the state rather than ends in themselves. He wrote:

> . . . .man is an end because he is a child of God. Man is not made for the state; the state is made for man. To deprive man of freedom is to relegate him to the status of a thing, rather than elevate him to the status of a person. Man must never be treated as a means to the end of the state, but always as an end within himself.[31]

King was correct in his assessment of the depersonalizing effects of segregation, particularly upon the victims. Oppression, however, also depersonalizes the oppressor. Since the days of antebellum slavery, right-thinking persons in the majority community have recognized the dehumanizing effects of oppression upon the victimizers. Persons cannot oppress one another without sacrificing something of their own humanity. When they oppress others, they limit their own sphere or capacity to love. The human heart has a natural inclination to love, which has been instilled within it by God. When violence is inflicted upon another human being or when another person is hated, the full and free expression of love is dramatically curtailed; pangs of conscience are felt within the heart. In order to come to grips with conscience, an individual or group may exercise one of at least two options: the natural predisposition to love can be suppressed until conscience is effectively silenced, or the object of violence and/or hate can be depersonalized.

The history of white America's dealings with black America has been for the most part one of depersonalization. During slavery blacks were written out of the human race altogether. Consequently, when the Society for the Propagation of the Gospel first proposed evangelizing black people, one of the issues that had to be decided was whether or not blacks even had souls to be saved. To admit the existence of the soul was to admit a quality of humanness, which had been denied. Later when black people were admitted to the human species by more progressive and liberal white thinkers, blacks were consigned to the category of subspecies, which was yet another form of depersonalization. The illogical/logical development of this school of thought was the definition of the Negro as being three-fifths of a man.

Racist white biblical scholars and fundamentalists provided theological legitimacy, as well as ecclesiological credibility, to the depersonalizing of blacks by misreading and misinterpreting Scripture to support the heresy of innate black inferiority. Blacks were said to be the descendants of the biblical character Ham, who was cursed by his father, Noah. As such, they were ordained by God to be hewers of wood, drawers of water, and servants. The tower of Babel story was not interpreted by whites as divine disapproval of human arrogance; rather, it was viewed as setting a divine mandate and precedent for segregation. Injunctions regarding master-servant relationships found in the Epistle to the Ephesians, and other passages credited to Pauline authorship, were understood by many whites as the New Testament blessing on the continued subjection of blacks to white domination.

The result of all of this theological and legal gerrymandering was the depersonalizing of blacks and the easing of the white conscience. King's own personal experiences with the dehumanizing effects of Jim Crow policies in the South, as well as his observations of the injustice inflicted upon black people, made him acutely aware of the destructive impact of racism upon the human personality. Consequently, a concept which identified personality as one of God's highest and most enduring gifts of the human spirit and as the essence of the *imago dei* would strike a responsive chord in the life and thought of an individual such as King, who was himself a victim of systemic depersonalization.

Further, King had been raised in a tradition which sought to counteract the damning effects of the white culture's depersonalization process. The black church has been the vehicle for the development of black personality. A statement often heard in black churches is that in the church, unlike the larger society, there are no "big I's and little you's." In other words, the church struggles to counteract the behavior pattern which elevates some while it depersonalizes others.

The black church is the setting where black talent is cultivated and where black people can function with a kind of autonomy and freedom which is often denied them in the larger society. More than one person has observed that the only boards on which a majority of black people sit are church boards—deacon boards; steward boards; stewardess, deaconess, and mothers' boards; trustee boards; and boards of ruling elders. Persons who hold menial jobs in the larger society, and who are looked through as if they don't exist or are looked down upon as if they have no right to exist, emerge as powerful personalities and individuals of influence within the black church. Janitors become policy-determining church officials; maids become presidents of influential church auxiliaries.

The effort to develop personality is one of the reasons that recognition is such an important aspect of black church life. Anyone who is part of the black church or who has attended black church functions will note the amount of time spent in calling the names of people and recognizing the various services and contributions rendered by the membership. Everyone from the cooks in the kitchen, the person who typed the program, to the larger contributors, is recognized. It is true that many persons consider these acts of recognition immature and a waste of time. However, one must recognize that this is one of the black church's many ways of building a sense of personal worth in those who must survive in a system which depersonalizes them every day of the week. When one functions in a society in which one's work is considered menial, in which one's being is hardly recognized, and in which one's name is not even known, then where does one receive recognition, have value attached to one's services, and worth ascribed to one's person but in the church? In a world of case load, Social Security, and insurance policy numbers, where else will one's name be known other than in the church? Black churches have understood that no one else will bestow upon their constituency the dignity of personality inherent in the human species.

The ministry of personalism, in a practical as well as theoretical way, has been and continues to be one of the essential ingredients of the ministry of the black church. It should be noted, however, that the recognition and development of personality is not intended to foster individualism in its pejorative sense. Personality is developed within the context of community. The black church as the community of faith, in response to its understanding of the *imago dei,* bestows upon the individual his or her own sense of positive self-understanding as a unique creation of God.

King grew up observing a practical theology which sought to lift human personalities out of the throes of a depersonalizing racist society and bestow upon these redeemed personalities the inherent dignity and freedom that God wills for humanity. King's own sense of personhood had been developed within the context of this black church tradition. Thus, his own experience in encountering the depersonalizing effects of racism and his religious heritage that sought to build personality were the linkages that fostered a kind of natural openness to the personalistic motifs presented to him by Davis at Crozer. These were further refined and solidified by Brightman and DeWolf at Boston University.

King's Doctrine of God: A Reflection of Personalism

Just as one cannot understand King without an awareness of black religion, so too one can have little understanding of King or his nonviolent ethic without an awareness of his doctrine of God. King's faith ultimately rested not in the power of nonviolence but in the power of God. King's nonviolent ethic was based upon the theological assumptions inherent in his doctrine of God. The personalism of Brightman at Boston helped King as he thought through this doctrine. Personalists assigned ultimate as well as ontological status to personality. As Smith and Zepp explained:

> This means, metaphysically speaking, that personality is the only adequate category available to describe God, the Supreme Cause of the universe and the only perfect personality. All finite personalities are faint copies of the Supreme Personality. According to this approach, the universe is a society of persons, and the central and most creative person is God.[32]

The personalism of Brightman became a metaphysical and philosophical rationale for theism in general. When combined with the evangelical liberal tradition, personalism became the metaphysical basis for the belief in the dignity and worth of all human personality and the philosophical foundation for the idea of a personal God.

The personalistic influence upon King was reflected in his dissertation, entitled "A Comparison of the Conceptions of God in the Thinking of Paul Tillich and Henry Nelson Wieman." He compared and contrasted the God concept as explicated by these two theologians. King chose the topic because of the centrality of the doctrine of God within any religious system and because of humanity's continued need to reinterpret and clarify the God concept. Tillich and Wieman were compared because of the different types of theology they represented and because of their influence upon theological and philosophical thought. [33]

After stating Tillich's and Wieman's theories both in terms of their methodologies and their conceptions of God, King's first conclusion was that both of them agreed that God is an undeniable reality. They were so convinced of the reality of God that they regarded all attempts to prove or argue logically for God's existence as futile and invalid. Both attempted to affirm the reality of God by defining God in such broad terms that denial of God's existence became virtually impossible. King, however, felt that in their attempts to define God in such a way, both Tillich and Wieman gave up much of that which is most essential for the idea of God from a religious point of view. He felt that both sacrificed too much for the sake of ridding themselves of the troublesome question of whether or not God existed.

Tillich's fundamental definition of God was *being itself*. God, for Tillich, was not a Being alongside other beings, but "being itself" or the power of being in everything and above everything. King's understanding of the Christian message was that God is a being, not "being itself." Although God is not a being along with others, but above others, the existence predicated of God differs qualitatively and quantitatively from the contingent, finite existence of God's creatures. God is not merely "the ground of everything personal"; God is personal.

Wieman's essential definition of God was *creative event*. "God as creative event is that process of reorganization which generates new meanings, integrates them with the old, and endows each event as it occurs with a wider range of reference." [34] He also defined God as *supreme value* and as "the unlimited connective growth of value-connections." King disagreed with Wieman's definitions because he believed that God was more than an impersonal process, event, or value operating within the natural sphere. He believed that God is a personal being, transcending nature and giving it meaning, coherence, and direction. King also questioned whether the existence of anything could be proved or affirmed simply by definition or the refinement of a concept.

Both Tillich and Wieman rejected personality as a category applicable to God. They felt that to refer to God as a person was to limit God; therefore, they used the term "supra-personal." King believed that "supra-personal" was, at best, a label for the unknown and a term without any content. People must conceive of God as either personal or impersonal. For King there was no third alternative. He felt that Tillich's and Wieman's contention that personality involved limitations rested on a false concept of the nature of personality. Although human personality is limited, there are no limitations inherent in the category of personality. Personality as such is simply self-consciousness and self-direction. King wrote:

> The idea of personality is so consistent with the notion of the Absolute that we must say with Bowne "that complete and perfect personality can be found only in the Infinite and Absolute Being, as only in him can we find that complete and perfect selfhood and self-expression which is necessary to the fulness of personality." The conception of God as personal, therefore, does not imply limitation of any kind.[35]

Tillich's and Wieman's conception of an impersonal God did not prevent them from endorsing the significant role of God as the symbol in religious worship. King believed these two assertions to be inconsistent. He questioned whether one could really worship a behavior process or an impersonal absolute. While the impersonal could be an object of thought, worship is a process of communion and intercourse between living minds. Therefore, before the impersonal could be worshiped, it would first have to be personalized. According to King, the religious man has always recognized two essential values—fellowship with God and trust in God's goodness—both of which presuppose and imply the personality of God. Interaction may exist between impersonal beings, but true fellowship cannot exist between impersonal beings. True fellowship is contingent upon freedom and intelligence and exists only between beings who know each other and who take a volitional attitude toward each other. It was inconceivable for King that communion with God could be possible if God were a mere "interaction" or "process," as Wieman believed, or "being itself," as Tillich asserted. "Fellowship," contended King, "requires an outgoing of feeling and will. This is what the Scripture means when it refers to God as the 'living' God. Life as applied to God means that in God there is feeling and will, responsive to the deepest yearnings of the human heart; this God both evokes and answers prayer."[36]

Both Tillich and Wieman believed in the goodness of God, but theirs was a goodness conceptualized in an abstract and impersonal sense rather than in a genuine ethical sense. King believed that goodness, like communion, presupposed freedom and intelligence and that only a personal being could be good. Thus, goodness is an attribute of personality. He made the same point about love. Although Tillich spoke of God as love and Wieman wrote about the need to love God, King felt that outside of personality, love loses its meaning. The object of love is a person, a concrete object, a persistent reality, and not mere interaction. A process or interaction may generate love, but love is not primarily directed toward the process but rather toward the persons who continue to generate the process. King responded to Tillich's and Wieman's denials of the category of personality to God by asserting:

> We must conclude that Tillich's "being-itself" and Wieman's "creative event" are lacking in positive religious value. Both concepts are too impersonal to express adequately the Christian conception of God. They provide neither the conditions for true fellowship with God nor the assurance of his goodness.[37]

King's interpretation of the nature of God differed from Tillich's and Wieman's in another major area of conceptualization. Interestingly, King also differed with Brightman on this same point. Tillich, Wieman, and Brightman were "finitistic theists." King was not. The assumption upon which Brightman based his concept of God's finitude was that a God who was both completely good and omnipotent would not allow evil. Since he believed that God was good, it followed that God could not be all-powerful. For Brightman, God's limitation was within an uncreated given aspect of God's nature. Like Brightman, Wieman stressed the goodness of God—for him, God was the only absolute good. He conceptualized the absolute good as having five qualities: (1) it is good under all circumstances and conditions;

(2) its demands are unlimited; (3) its value is infinite; (4) its goodness is unqualified; and (5) it is entirely trustworthy. For Wieman, God meets all the requirements in that the goodness is not relative to time, place, desire, or human existence; God demands our wholehearted commitment and is entirely trustworthy. God's worth is not commensurable with any finite quality of created good, nor is there any perspective from which God's goodness can be modified. As the absolute good, God is the source only of good; thus God is limited by evil forces external to God's nature. For Wieman the very existence of evil means that God cannot be the ultimate ground of all existence.

While Wieman stressed God's goodness, Tillich stressed God's power. God, for Tillich, is the power of being which resists and conquers nonbeing. It is because of this power to resist nonbeing that God warrants ultimate human allegiance and concern. Omnipotence for Tillich did not mean that God has the power to do anything God wishes; it did not mean unrestricted power in terms of creation *ex nihilo* or causality; nor did it mean power over evil. Omnipotence for Tillich meant the power of being which resists nonbeing in all of its manifestations. Tillich dealt with the existence of evil by positing a nonrational aspect in God's nature known as "abyss." It is this nonrational aspect of God's nature which accounts for much of the evil in the world. Thus, Tillich, like Wieman and Brightman, ended up with a God who is also finite.

King distinguished Tillich's concept of God's finitude from Wieman's by stating that in Wieman's thought the limitation of God's power is external to God's nature, while in Tillich's thought the limitation is an aspect within God's nature.

King felt that Tillich and Wieman were both right and wrong. They were correct in what they affirmed and wrong in what they denied. Tillich was right in affirming God's power, but wrong in minimizing God's goodness. Wieman was right in affirming God's goodness but wrong in minimizing God's power. Both overemphasized one aspect of God's nature while neglecting another significant aspect of it. It is not a matter of God being either powerful *or* good; it is a matter of God being powerful *and* good. Thus, King could write:

> Value in itself is impotent. Hence a God devoid of power is ultimately

incapable of actualizing the good. But if God is truly God and warrants man's ultimate devotion, he must have not only an infinite concern for the good but an infinite power to actualize the good.[38]

It is power that gives reality to divine being. King interpreted divine omnipotence as the power of God to realize the good and to accomplish the divine purpose. King believed that without a corresponding and sustaining power, moral perfection would be void of meaning.

King's Doctrine of God: A Reflection of Black Religion

King's doctrine of God reflected not only the influence of personalism but also the theological insights of black religion. Traditionally black religion has been able to balance and hold in tension the suffering of black people in one hand and God's goodness and omnipotence in the other. Even though black people have not always been able to answer adequately the "why" question inherent in the matter of theodicy, the question has not driven blacks, for the most part, to a denial of God's existence, God's goodness, God's justice, or God's power.

For example, in spite of their suffering or maybe because of it, blacks have maintained a belief in the existence and the goodness of God. In the midst of this "veil of tears" and this "mean and unfriendly world," which has shown itself capable of crushing the aspirations of those who pass through it, blacks have been made painfully aware of their lack of power and control. They have not, however, resigned themselves to their plight nor as a people become fatalists. Blacks have recognized that "though troubled on every side, they have not been distressed; though perplexed, they have not been driven to despair; though persecuted, they have not been forsaken; though cast down, they have not been destroyed" (see 2 Corinthians 4:8-9, KJV). The paradigm for their suffering has been the biblical character Job, who, though he questioned God, did not curse God. Neither did Job allow others to impose a line of reasoning upon him which stated that his suffering was due to his own sins and weaknesses. Blacks are aware that they have not simply survived and endured their troubles. Rather, they have emerged triumphant with integrity of soul and spirit because they have been cared for by a loving God who is personal.

In traditional black religious thought God is a being with personality, who can be loved as well as rejected, praised and worshiped as well as denied. When forces of dehumanization and oppression are confronted daily, when the environment is perceived essentially as hostile rather than supportive, blacks must have a God who personally cares for them, who hears their cries, understands their sorrows, and assures them of divine presence and help in times of need and distress.

The caring aspect of God's personality is reflected in the characterization often used in black religious circles that "God is a mother to the motherless, and a father to the fatherless." What is significant in this characterization is its appropriateness for the black predicament, personally and corporately. With the assault of slavery upon the structure and stability of the black family, a number of blacks were, in fact, orphaned. The church became the family for many of these persons. God was perceived as the head of the family. So in their churches blacks learned about a family head who was both mother and father to them. Corporately, blacks were cut off from their cultural and historical African roots and never wholly incorporated or accepted as full members and participants in their new environment. In a culture in which blacks never felt completely at home at best, and completely alienated at worst, due to racial hostility, many did feel like motherless children "a long ways from home." However, black religion taught them that there was Somebody—which denotes personality—who cares for them, even in "a strange land," and that this caring personality is God.

In the traditional black religious perspective, the good God with a caring heart also has a strong arm of protection. God's care is matched by God's infinite and eternal resources of assistance. Blacks are not finitistic theists. The caring-powerful dimension of God is demonstrated in one of the great sermons that has emerged from the black religious experience. Traditionally known as "The Eagle Stirreth Her Nest," the sermon is appropriate for a number of reasons. In addition to the mother eagle (the female image) in the sermon being a characterization of God, the eagle also has a personality, manifested in its stirring its nest as a method of training its offspring. The eagle as conceptualized is not only a caring creature but also a bird that represents power. The mother eagle's capacity for tenderness is matched by her tremendous strength. Black religion has used the eagle as an archetype of the way that tenderness and strength coexist in God. Black preachers have used the eagle's process of stirring its nest as symptomatic of the way trials are used to benefit God's children. As the eagle stirs her nest and makes it uncomfortable, encouraging the young to learn to fly and to leave, so trials which afflict and discomfort become the means by which God's children test their wings of faith and their capacity to endure. Throughout the whole process God's children are sustained, encouraged, and supported by the power of God.

The God of tenderness and strength is the God who delivered the children of Israel from Egyptian bondage, the Hebrew boys from the fiery furnace, and Daniel from the lions' den. This is the God who placed Esther on the throne for a time of intercession and who, according to the prophetess Deborah, arranged the stars in their courses to fight against Sisera. Blacks have had a particular affinity for these Old Testament liberation and deliverance narratives. They saw their plight in the biblical stories and believed that as God had delivered the Jews in Old Testament times, God could and would deliver them from their oppressors.

It is to be noted that black faith is based not in human, but in divine resources. Traditionally, black thinking has not been as optimistic regarding the innate goodness of human nature as liberalism has been. The oppressed, the victimized, and those at the bottom are the victims of human sin. Being a victim gives one a different perspective of life. In regard to human nature, traditional black religious thought has been closer to the neo-orthodoxy of Reinhold Niebuhr than to liberalism. Even Martin King, who affirmed so many of the themes of evangelical liberalism, had difficulty in accepting its view of human nature. While at Crozer, King wrote:

> At one time I find myself leaning toward a mild neo-orthodox view of man. The former learning may root back in certain experiences that I had in the South with a vicious race problem. Some of the experiences that I encountered there made it very difficult for me to believe in the essential goodness of man.[39]

Martin King as an oppressed person could not accept liberalism's view of the inherent goodness of human nature. His own experience as a Southern black gave him a perspective which many evangelical liberals did not have. However, King was not driven to despair, for, like many other blacks, he had faith in God. King's theology reflected the teachings of traditional black religion: God is a being with personality who embodies both tenderness and strength and who can thus make ways out of no ways as well as wipe the tears from a child's eyes.

In a rather long but moving passage in *Strength to Love*, King stated clearly his doctrine of God. This doctrine of God was more than an intellectual formulation; it was one which emerged out of King's own trials. He wrote:

> The agonizing moments through which I have passed during the last few years have also drawn me closer to God. More than ever before I am convinced of the reality of a personal God. True, I have always believed in the personality of God. But in the past the idea of a personal God was little more than a metaphysical category that I found theologically and philosophically satisfying. Now it is a living reality that has been validated in the experiences of everyday life. God has been profoundly real to me in recent years. In the midst of lonely days and dreary nights I have heard an inner voice saying, "Lo, I will be with you." When the chains of fear and the manacles of frustration have all but stymied my efforts, I have felt the power of God transforming the fatigue of despair into the buoyancy of hope. I am convinced that the universe is under the control of a loving purpose, and that in the struggle for righteousness man has cosmic companionship. Behind the harsh appearances of the world there is a benign power. To say that this God is personal is not to make him a finite object beside other objects or attribute to him the limitations of human personality; it is to take what is finest and noblest in our consciousness and affirm its perfect existence in him. It is certainly true that human personality is limited, but personality as such involves no necessary limitations. It means simply self-consciousness and self-direction. So in the truest sense of the word, God is a living God. In him there is feeling and will, responsive to the deepest yearnings of the human heart. This God both evokes and answers prayer.[40]

Summary

In his theological and ethical perspective King affirmed a number of other themes whose foundations were rooted in black religion and which were reinforced by the insights of evangelical liberalism. It is evident, then, that black religion was one of the major formative sources for King's intellectual development. By the time he studied at Crozer Seminary and at Boston University, King already had an openness and proclivity to such motifs as the existence of a moral order, the action of God in history, the social character of existence, and personalism, since these themes were embraced by black religion. He had difficulty accepting liberalism's belief in the inherent goodness of human nature and disagreed with some evangelical liberals who believed that God's goodness and omnipotence could not be held in balance, or in tension, in the face of evil. On those points King agreed with the viewpoint of traditional black religious thought, which took a less positive view of human nature and which insisted that, the existence of evil notwithstanding, God is still good and all-powerful.

2

From Tactic to Way of Life: King's Personal Odyssey with Nonviolence

The story of Martin King's career as a prophet of social justice is also the story of his personal odyssey with nonviolence, philosophically and methodologically. King's nonviolent ethic developed along two concomitant lines—as a method of social protest and as a philosophy of life. Although the development of these two strands was essentially a concurrent process—evolving out of a common milieu of struggle, experimentation, and experiences with nonviolence—here they shall be treated separately.

Martin Luther King did not emerge in full bloom from the Montgomery bus boycott experience as America's foremost nonviolent theorist and practitioner. His adoption of nonviolence as a way of life was a matured perspective. He had reached the conclusion that nonviolence would be an appropriate strategy for international relationships, as well as a viable and effective vehicle for the redressing of domestic social problems on a national scale. This conclusion was reached as his ethic had been tested and honed by experience and fire in Alabama, Georgia, Mississippi, Florida, Tennessee, the large and complex urban centers of the North, and the peace movement. King's perspective had withstood attacks against his reputation as well as his physical person. It had been debated in late-night and early-morning discussions as well as in mid-afternoon classes and retreats. It had been debated by King's colleagues and a younger generation of committed and thoughtful black women and men who pondered the theoretical foundations of nonviolence both as a philosophy and as a strategy.

From his first readings of Gandhi's works, to his first experience with nonviolence as a vehicle of protest, to the day he was assassinated, nonviolence for King continued to be an evolving phenomenon, a fluid process rather than a static system. The roots of King's search for a viable method of social protest for black Americans are found in the days of his adolescence when he had his own psychologically assaultive experiences with racism. As he observed the suffering of his people, he began to think of a way to redress the injustice borne out of the racism he saw. At Morehouse College, the black institution that served as the foundation for his graduate and professional education in a course taught by Professor Samuel Williams, he had been introduced to the first intellectual source of his developing ethical consciousness: Henry David Thoreau's "Essay on Civil Disobedience." Thoreau's concept of not cooperating with an evil system so fascinated young King that he reread the essay several times.

The Influence of Gandhi

At Crozer Theological Seminary, after graduating from Morehouse, King continued his formal preparation for the Christian ministry and his quest for a viable method of social protest and change for America's oppressed blacks. Although he had heard of Gandhi before, it was in the spring of 1950, when he was a seminarian, that King really "discovered" Gandhism in terms of its potential for social change. One Sunday afternoon, King traveled to Philadelphia, Pennsylvania, to hear Dr. Mordecai Johnson, president of Howard University, preach for the Fellowship House of Philadelphia. Dr. Johnson had recently returned from a trip to India and, consequently, to King's great interest, spoke on the life and teachings of Mahatma Gandhi. According to Dr. Johnson, Gandhi had done five things, any one of which would have been enough to earn him greatness: (1) Gandhi had freed India of British rule; (2) he had done so without either committing a violent act or uttering a violent word; (3) Gandhi had championed the cause of the Untouchables, bringing them into the pool of acceptability within the Hindu society and culture; (4) Gandhi had lived an ascetic life of poverty, simplicity, and reflection; and (5) he had demonstrated the uses and potential of love as a force within movements of social and political reform.[1]

It was the last point, that of the potential of love as a means of nonviolent social reform, which struck King as having possibilities for his own intellectual search for a method of social change. He saw it as both viable for black Americans and consistent with his understanding of the teachings of Jesus. King was so impressed and affected by Dr. Johnson's speech that he left the meeting and bought a half dozen books on Gandhi. He was fascinated by Gandhi's campaigns of nonviolence. He was particularly moved by the Salt March and Gandhi's numerous fasts. The whole concept of *satyagraha* (truth-force, love-force or soul-force) took on a special significance for him. For King, love (*agape*) described the essence of the ethics, or teachings, of Jesus. As a black Christian, King desired a method of social change which was grounded in and consistent with the faith in which he and the bulk of black Americans had been nurtured. Heretofore, King had been frustrated in his intellectual search for a viable method of social change because the love which Jesus taught and exemplified seemed applicable only to individual relationships with few or no possibilities for application in the realm of social change.

In his reading of Gandhi's works, King not only gained new insight into and a deeper appreciation of Gandhi and his ideas, but he also began to see the potential of the teachings and ethic of Jesus for social change. As he delved deeper into the philosophy of Gandhi, King's skepticism about the power of love diminished, and for the first time he began to understand its potency and potential for social change. King later wrote:

Prior to reading Gandhi, I had about concluded that the ethics of Jesus were only effective in individual relationship. The "turn the other cheek" philosophy and the "love your enemies" philosophy were only valid, I felt, when individuals were in conflict with other individuals; when racial groups and nations were in conflict a more realistic approach seemed necessary. But after reading Gandhi, I saw how utterly mistaken I was.[2]

This new appraisal of the ethics of Jesus, gleaned from his fresh discovery of Gandhi's thought, had a decided impact upon King's thought. He began to believe that he had finally found the key by which the oppressed could unlock the door of social protest. In Gandhism King found a way to fight the oppression of black Americans, and the method was consistent with the Christian ethic of love as he understood it. According to King:

> Gandhi was probably the first person in history to lift the love ethic of Jesus above mere interaction between individuals to a powerful and effective social force on a large scale. For Gandhi love was a potent instrument for social and collective transformation. It was in this Gandhian emphasis on love and nonviolence that I discovered the method for social reform that I had been seeking for so many months. . . . I came to feel that this was the only morally and practically sound method open to oppressed people in their struggle for freedom.[3]

One notes that for King love as a force within nonviolence was as significant as the nonviolent methodology itself. What was important to King was not simply Gandhian nonviolence, but King's understanding of Gandhian nonviolence in terms of the love ethic of Jesus. It is possible that one of the reasons King so readily appropriated the love motif in Gandhism is that love is one of the great themes of traditional black preaching. Hate, manifested both as self-deprecation or self-loathing and hostility toward those of the majority or oppressing community, is an emotion which the oppressed know all too well. It can easily grip a person as one reflects historically about the pain and hardships that one's forebears underwent. That same hate can easily grip an individual engaged in his or her own fights against the daily onslaughts of personal and institutional racism.

Traditionally, black preachers have been aware of how easily hate can grip and harden the hearts and spirits of black people. This is why black congregations are constantly exhorted to "love your enemies, do good to them which hate you, bless them that curse you, and pray for them which despitefully use you" (Luke 6:27-28). This exhortation can also be directed toward those brothers and sisters within the oppressed community or church family who have wronged one another. However, the exhortation to love has particular relevance to the broader world of work and business where the oppressed are exposed to racism in its most raw and brutal forms. It is in this broader world, the world which is structured and controlled by whites, where blacks are made to feel like aliens, that the temptation to hate is strongest. For the sake of their own survival, as well as the well-being of their minds and souls, blacks must participate in the broader world with the exhortation ringing in their ears as a constant reminder, "Love your enemies. . . ." Therefore, King may have had a natural inclination to identify the love ethic of Jesus in Gandhian nonviolence based upon how that love had been emphasized in traditional black preaching and fostered and demonstrated in the black church.

Thus, King's personal odyssey with nonviolence began while he was still a student, first at Morehouse College and then at Crozer Seminary, as he sought a viable Christian method of social protest for America's oppressed blacks. His roots in the black church continued to sensitize him to certain themes within the sources which he would one day use in the development and application of his nonviolent ethic. However, one would be mistaken if one concluded that King graduated from Crozer and then later from Boston University as a budding young social reformer with a neatly packaged theory of social protest which only needed an appropriate place and opportunity for its application. It would not be until years later that the seeds planted by Mordecai Johnson would really begin to bear fruit in the life and career of Martin Luther King, Jr.

The first significant introduction of Martin King to Gandhi was unexpected. The first opportunity that King would have to apply the love ethic of Jesus and the Gandhian principles of nonviolence in a situation of social reform and protest also came unexpectedly. It began on December 1, 1955, in Montgomery, Alabama, when Mrs. Rosa Parks, a seamstress who was black and whose feet were tired, was arrested for refusing to give up her seat (which was inside the designated area for persons of color) to a white male passenger. Journalist Louis Lomax has said that "the Negro revolt is properly dated from the moment Mrs. Parks said 'no' to the bus driver's demand that she get up and let a white man have her seat."[4] King said that

Mrs. Parks was ideal for the role assigned to her by history. She was a charming person with a radiant personality, soft spoken and calm in all situations. Her character was impeccable and her dedication deep-rooted. All of these traits together made her one of the most respected people in the Negro community.[5]

The arrest of Mrs. Parks, the subsequent events, the movement which developed out of those events, and the personalities who were shaped by those events and who gave leadership to the movement affected both directly and indirectly the lives of millions of Americans and touched the very soul of America. According to Lerone Bennett:

Rosa Parks's arrest did what no other event, however horrible, had been able to do: it unified and focused the discontent of the entire Negro community. By doing this, by proving that it could be done, the arrest released dammed-up deposits of social energy that rolled across the face of the South and the North. There was, first of all and most important of all, a one-day boycott. The one-day boycott stretched out to 382 days. The 382 days changed the spirit of Martin King, Jr., and King, thus transformed, helped to change the face and the heart of the Negro, of the white man, and of America.[6]

The Montgomery bus boycott had the greatest impact upon the life of young King, who had recently completed work on his Ph.D. degree at Boston University and had moved to Montgomery as the pastor of Dexter Avenue Baptist Church. On a social level, Montgomery has been viewed by some as a sensitizing symbol and "myth event" comparable, in a different era and on a smaller scale, to the French Revolution.[7] On a personal level, it has to be seen as the launching pad for the civil rights career of Martin Luther King. He was catapulted into orbit before he knew what was happening.

Once he had a quiet moment to reflect and assess his life, it was too late. He had gained international fame, the applause of the world was ringing in his ears, eighteen million Negroes were calling him "Savior" and world ethicists were comparing him to Gandhi and Thoreau.[8]

There are many factors which separate Montgomery from King's other campaigns. Lionel Lokos, one of King's more severe critics, has pointed out that in the other campaigns King and his associates were outsiders reinforcing local residents of the target city which was to come under nonviolent siege. In Montgomery, King and his associates were the local leaders who headed a campaign composed of other local residents. In other campaigns civil disobedience was encouraged and practiced. In Montgomery there was no civil disobedience. Montgomery, for Lokos, was a boycott pure and simple, and not the act of massive noncooperation that King considered it to be. In the other campaigns, there was a mixture of religious and secular groups, moderate and radical elements, and student representation and participation. In Montgomery, almost the entire movement was under the direction and control of the clergy. In other campaigns King invariably called for federal assistance, intervention, and legislation. In Montgomery, however, the primary goal was to bring about a local solution to a local problem.[9]

One should not forget that Martin King did not go to Montgomery, Alabama, to become a social reformer. He went to Montgomery to pastor the Dexter Avenue Baptist Church. The role of nonviolent theorist and practitioner, social prophet, and spokesperson for America's oppressed was unexpected. His election as the president of the Montgomery Improvement Association, the organization which directed the spontaneous movement, was unexpected. As a new pastor in town, King had not become linked with any of the local leadership factions, nor had he become allied with any one civic or political group. Thus, he was seen even at the onset as a unifying symbol. If there is any one characteristic which defined the Montgomery movement, it was spontaneity in the sense of the unexpected. No one anticipated the gentle and soft-spoken Rosa Parks's action in refusing to yield her seat to a white male as she sat within the designated boundaries for black passengers on the local segregated bus. No one anticipated that it would be the arrest of Rosa Parks, the proverbial last straw in a long series of abuses borne by the black community, which would ignite the flame of revolt within it and mobilize it for concerted action. No one anticipated that a one-day boycott would stretch into a 382-day boycott which would end in a U.S. Supreme Court decision declaring segregation statutes of Montgomery buses to be unconstitutional. No one anticipated the national focus that would be turned on Montgomery blacks and their leadership as they sought to resolve a local problem. No one foresaw the significance of their actions and victory in challenging racism in all of its manifestations across America. No one anticipated the emergence of

Martin Luther King, Jr., as a latter-day "Moses" or as the "American Gandhi" for this nation's liberal constituencies, politically and theologically, in both the black and the white communities. Even the victory came at an unexpected time and in an unexpected way. A significant part of the daily operation of the boycott was a car pool of more than three hundred vehicles that moved with "military precision." Various attempts were made to prevent the carpool from operating, including insurance companies (stating that the risk was too high) canceling the policies on some of the cars. However, a London company agreed to insure those cars on which policies had been canceled. The greatest challenge to the car pool and possibly to the boycott itself came when the city of Montgomery took legal action against the car pool. The threat which the city's injunction posed to the boycott was expressed by King when he wrote of speaking to the people to tell them that the car pool would probably be enjoined:

> The night before the hearing I had to go before the mass meeting to warn the people that the car pool would probably be enjoined. I knew that they had willingly suffered for nearly twelve months, but how could they function at all with the car pool destroyed? Could we ask them to walk back and forth every day to their jobs? And if not, would we then be forced to admit that the protest had failed in the end? For the first time in our long struggle together, I almost shrank from appearing before them. [10]

King attempted to bolster the spirits of his followers, but in spite of his words he still felt a cold breeze of pessimism passing through the audience. He wrote: "It was a dark night—darker than a thousand midnights. It was a night in which the light of hope was about to fade away and the lamp of faith about to flicker. We went home with nothing before us but a cloud of uncertainty." [11]

The next day King's suspicions were confirmed. The car pool was enjoined. However, before the judge's decision was rendered, the news of the Supreme Court's ruling, which upheld the decision of the U.S. District Court that had declared Alabama's segregated bus policy both on state and local levels was unconstitutional, had reached Montgomery. Thus the judge's ruling was anticlimactic, and the effects of it upon the boycott were made void by the decision of the nation's highest court. When the blacks in the Montgomery courtroom were informed of the Supreme Court's decision, one bystander said that "God almighty has spoken from Washington, D.C." King wrote that

Tuesday, November 13, 1956, will remain an important and ironic date in the history of the Montgomery bus protest. On that day two historic decisions were rendered—one to do away with the pool; the other to remove the underlying conditions that made it necessary. [12]

Just a Tactic

A casual reading of the Montgomery story will further reveal that at the beginning of the struggle, the basic philosophy for King and his constituency was Christian love, as they understood it, rather than Gandhism. King himself stated that at the beginning of the boycott the theoretical framework of the movement was shaped by the protesters' understanding and interpretation of the love ethic of Jesus:

From the beginning a basic philosophy guided the movement. This guiding principle has since been referred to variously as nonviolent resistance, noncooperation, and passive resistance. But in the first days of the protest none of these expressions was mentioned; the phrase most often heard was "Christian love." It was the Sermon on the Mount, rather than a doctrine of passive resistance, that initially inspired the Negroes of Montgomery to dignified social action. It was Jesus of Nazareth that stirred the Negroes to protest with the creative weapon of love. [13]

Like so much of the Montgomery movement, the first public mention of Gandhi in relationship to the boycott came from an unexpected source. About a week after the boycott began, Miss Juliette Morgan, a Southern white woman, wrote a letter to the *Montgomery Advertiser* in which she pointed out the similarities between the bus boycott and Gandhi's crusade. King and all the other leaders who were beginning to move in a similar direction seized upon this cue from this unexpected source and began to use Gandhi as an authority in their frequent appeals for restraint. King in reflection upon the early days of the boycott wrote:

As the days unfolded, however, the inspiration of Mahatma Gandhi began to exert its influence. I had come to see early that the Christian doctrine of love operating through the Gandhian method of nonviolence was one of the most potent weapons available to the Negro in his struggle for freedom. . . . Nonviolent resistance. . . . emerged as the technique of the movement, while love stood as the regulating ideal. In other words, Christ furnished the spirit and motivation, while Gandhi furnished the method.[14]

It is significant that King considered Gandhi's contribution to the Montgomery bus boycott to be methodological in nature. King first viewed nonviolence only as a strategy or method for social change and was not ready to embrace the nonviolent philosophy as a way of life. Gandhi, for example, not only refrained from physical acts of violence but also avoided violence of the spirit. The person for whom nonviolence has become a way of life not only must refuse to strike a perpetrator of violence but also must refuse to hate. During the Montgomery bus boycotts, as well as at other times, King had to struggle with his own potential for hate. His writings occasionally mentioned how certain incidents and experiences drove him perilously close to hate.

In the midst of the boycott, King's house was bombed, and although his wife and daughter were in the house when the explosion occurred, they were not harmed. Later that night in the safety of a church member's home, King thought about what could have happened to his wife and daughter, and he could feel the emotion of hate welling up in his heart.

When one reads of this and other incidents, one realizes that King really had to come to grips with and struggle with his own potential for hate. King knew firsthand, from his own personal odyssey with nonviolence, how easy it is to hate and how destructive hate can be to the human spirit. After the bombing, upon the urging of friends, King applied for a license to carry a handgun in the car. The application was denied and as King later reflected on the matter, he came to the conclusion that it was inconsistent for a person to serve as a leader of a nonviolent movement and at the same time use weapons of violence for his own personal protection. Nonviolence, however, had still not become a personal philosophy. Once, during a television interview, the black American journalist Louis Lomax asked King what he would do if someone, white or black, entered his home and menaced his wife and children. King replied: "Louis, I don't know what I would do; my advocacy of nonviolence is as a tactic during demonstrations, not as a total private way of life."[15]

From Assent to Actuality

In 1957 King began, in the words of the prophet Isaiah, to "lengthen his cords and strengthen his stakes" in terms of his own involvement and commitment to nonviolence. Before this time he had had an intellectual commitment to nonviolence which did not require much physical suffering. He was criticized by some black leaders when he first started preaching nonviolence and talking about Gandhi because of his detached intellectual commitment. Even later in his career as a civil rights leader, King received criticism from various sources about the extent of his personal suffering and the differences between his style of leadership and that of Gandhi. During the era of the freedom riders in the 1960s, Robert Williams, a local NAACP leader in North Carolina, wired an ultimatum to King that stated:

> The cause of human decency and black liberation demands that you physically ride the buses with our gallant Freedom Riders. No sincere leader asks his followers to make sacrifices that he himself will not endure. You are a phony. Gandhi was always in the forefront, suffering with his people. If you are the leader of this movement, lead the way by example.[16]

King began to think about the broader dimensions of nonviolence, including the matter of his own personal physical suffering and sacrifice. In mid-August 1957, the Gandhian scholar and disciple Ranganath Diwaker paid a three-day visit to King in Montgomery. During his visit, Diwaker convinced King that he, too, must set an example of physical suffering. Up to this point much of King's agony had been mental. Coretta King said of this period that "we began to think about how superficial and shallow our knowledge of the whole thing was."[17] King resolved that the next time he was given the choice of either paying a fine or accepting imprisonment, he would choose imprisonment.

King was unexpectedly given the opportunity to implement his resolve on September 3 of that year. On that day he and his wife went to the Montgomery courthouse where King's colleague Ralph Abernathy was to testify in a private case. King was standing with some other persons in a group just outside the courtroom when a policeman ordered them to move along. King said, "I am waiting to see my lawyer, Fred Gary." The policeman replied, "If you don't get the hell out of here, you're going to need a lawyer." When King stood his ground, the officer said, "Boy, you done it now." Another policeman was called, and he pushed King toward city hall. As King's wife followed behind him, the policeman said to her, "You want to go to jail, too, gal? Just nod your head if you want to." King, looking over his shoulder at his wife, said, "Don't say anything, darling." King was then taken to the city hall where he was kicked and roughed up. Then, when his identity was learned, he was charged with disobeying an officer and released on his own recognizance.

Upon his arrival home, King had a long talk with his wife. Knowing that he would be convicted and fined, he said to her, "The time has come when I should no longer accept bails. If I commit a crime in the name of civil rights, I will go to jail and serve the time." When King was tried, found guilty, and sentenced to a fine of ten dollars or fourteen days in jail, he asked the judge permission to make a statement in which he stated his choice of going to jail. King's action surprised the judge, who recessed the court and then said to him, "Dr. King, you know you can get out on bail. Wouldn't you like to get someone to pay your fine?" King answered, "No, your honor, I do not wish to pay the fine." Mrs. King, writing about this incident, said:

> Martin was responding to the influence of Gandhi and his technique of noncooperation. But my husband was becoming firmly convinced that the black leadership must prepare to suffer as Gandhi had. He did not want to go to jail; it was a terrible prospect for a man as sensitive and fastidious as he. . . . However, Martin realized that his imprisonment would arouse sympathy for our Movement. He felt that if he asked other people to suffer in the cause, then he, their leader, should be prepared to do so in still greater measure.[18]

King, however, was denied in this instance the opportunity of serving time in jail. When the time came for him to go to jail, he was told to go home because someone had paid his fine. When King asked who his benefactor was, he was told that it was probably one of his associates. King insisted that this could not be the case since he had informed his associates of his plans and had specifically instructed them not to pay his fine. When King persisted in his inquiry, he was told that an anonymous donor had paid the fine. Finally, one of King's greatest adversaries in the Montgomery bus boycott, Police Commissioner Clyde Sellers, issued a statement that he had paid the fine out of his own pocket to prevent King from using the jail "for his own selfish purposes" and "to save the taxpayers the expense of feeding King for fourteen days."

Although King was denied this opportunity to spend time in jail, he was not denied others. What is important to note is King's decision, based upon Gandhian influence and a maturing personal commitment to nonviolence, to go to jail rather than pay the fine. Beginning with this incident in Montgomery in 1957, for the remainder of his life, whenever he was given a choice of paying a fine or serving time, whether it was in Montgomery, Albany, Birmingham, or Selma, King chose jail, although there were instances when he did not serve the full sentences.

In February 1959 King, his wife, Coretta, and one of his biographers, Professor Lawrence Reddick, made a pilgrimage to India. During the visit, King had the opportunity to discuss not only Gandhian nonviolence but also other aspects of Gandhism with the men who had worked and suffered with Gandhi and who had applied his philosophy to the struggles of their nation as well as to their own lives. The visit to India further strengthened King's belief in the potential of nonviolence for reconciliation. In his opinion the aftermath of hatred and bitterness which usually follows a violent campaign of liberation was not found in India. According to King, a new relationship based on complete equality had been established between the Indian and the British people within the Commonwealth.

The impact of his visit to India was such that it not only made King think more deeply about the nonviolent philosophy, per se, but also caused him to reexamine his values and his style of living. He returned to America more determined than ever to live as simply as possible. Coretta King, in describing the way that the pilgrimage to India affected King personally as well as philosophically, wrote:

> Martin returned from India more devoted than ever to Gandhian ideals and simplicity of living. He constantly pondered how to apply them in America. His great problem was the enormous difference between the mechanized complexity of our way of living and theirs . . . . He felt, as in India, that much of the corruption in our society stems from the desire to acquire material things—houses and land and cars. Martin would have preferred to have none of these things.[19]

Although King may have preferred to live a simpler, more ascetic existence, he recognized that in his civilization and culture a person could not function without a place to live; communication would be extremely difficult without the telephone; and anyone who had to travel would be adversely affected without an automobile. So he decided to seek kinship with Gandhi spiritually rather than materially or physically. If King and Gandhi didn't and couldn't have similar lifestyles, if the physical circumstances in which they found themselves were different, then perhaps they could still have similar approaches to and understanding of nonviolence in spite of their differing contexts. Nonviolence for Gandhi was a way of life. In time King did achieve a type of spiritual kinship with Gandhi when he, too, accepted nonviolence as a way of life. In *Stride Toward Freedom* King wrote: "Admittedly, nonviolence in the truest sense is not a strategy that one uses simply because it is expedient at the moment; nonviolence is ultimately a way of life that men live by because of the sheer morality of its claim."[20] Attesting the thoroughness of her husband's conversion, Coretta King stated:

> In the early years, when he first preached nonviolence, Martin would be asked the inevitable question put to all men of his belief, "What would you do if someone were attacking your wife?" He would answer them, "I am not sure. But I hope that I would not respond with violence." Later, as his ideals of nonviolence were tested in fire, he was able to answer more surely, confident out of his terrible experiences, that he would not strike out.[21]

King's personal odyssey with nonviolence developed from his initial intellectual recognition of its potential as a means of social protest and reform for America's oppressed blacks, to its uses as a strategy, to its adoption as a personal way of life. This conversion was not only the result of the deeper insights he gained as he learned more and more about Gandhian nonviolence; much of that conversion process occurred through King's own experiments with the truth of nonviolence, as he lived it, applied it, refined it, and suffered through it, beginning in Montgomery. Later, reflecting on the Montgomery struggle in terms of its meaning for his own personal odyssey with nonviolence, King wrote:

> The experience in Montgomery did more to clarify my thinking in regard to the question of nonviolence than all of the books I had read. As the days unfolded, I became more and more convinced of the power of nonviolence. Nonviolence became more than a method

to which I gave intellectual assent; it became a commitment to a way of life.[22]

We shall now turn our attention to the detailed application of King's ethic. This application was more than a refinement and expansion of its uses and the contexts in which the ethic could be applied. It was also part of King's continuing personal odyssey with nonviolence.

3

The Developing Ethic: Albany, Birmingham, Selma

At the same time that King's commitment to nonviolence as a philosophy of life was being strengthened, his understanding of nonviolence as a vehicle of social protest, along with his skills in its usage, was also being developed in the crucible of human experience and experimentation. The Montgomery experience was significant for King's personal development as well as that of his nonviolent ethic. The Montgomery bus boycott was King's initial attempt at social protest, and as previously stated, it was unanticipated. It was an attempt that was without precedent and without study or preparation. There had been no prior mobilization and organization of the black community to examine, as was possible in some of the later campaigns. The Montgomery experience, therefore, was without the wisdom that only comes with experience. Persons who are overly critical of the Montgomery bus boycott and of King's leadership would do well to remember that it was a first attempt and also that the South in the decade before the 1960s was a different place from what it is now.

Before 1960, the whole of America was not sensitive to the

plight of blacks in the South. Thus, the Montgomery bus boycott, when viewed in the proper context of time and place, was looked upon as a bold and audacious step by the black community. Martin Luther King, Jr., was regarded by a number of persons in the white community at the time as a radical because of his involvement and leadership. Montgomery awakened America as a nation to the cancerous growth called racism that was destroying the aspirations of a large segment of its people. Montgomery, then, provided King with his initial experience in the use of a nonviolent strategy. King also had his initial confrontation with institutional racism as represented by hostile and intransigent local officials. Montgomery was also the place where the transformation of Martin Luther King, Jr., from pastor to prophet of social injustice began to take place.

In the early days of the movement, subsequent to the Montgomery victory, King was very cautious in advocating that blacks in other communities engage in similar campaigns. He stated:

> All cities have conditions that could lead to the kind of thing we are doing in Montgomery. I would not, however, advocate the indiscriminate use of the boycott as a weapon. When it is tried, the Negro must be sure that it is well organized, strategically wise, and in an area where counter-boycotts cannot be used against them.[1]

However, in his last book, *The Trumpet of Conscience*, King said, "Nonviolent protest must now mature to a new level to correspond to heightened black impatience and stiffened white resistance. This higher level is mass civil disobedience."[2] He not only advocated "a sustained, direct-action movement of civil disobedience on a national scale," but also stated that the next stage of the movement was to become international.[3] To understand how King's journey led him from a cautious advocacy of the boycott on the local level to a call for massive civil disobedience on a national scale and the application of nonviolence to international areas of conflict and tension, one must understand the process of constant rethinking, reshaping, and reworking that King's ethic of nonviolence underwent as it was "tested by fire" in the battles of Montgomery, Albany, Birmingham, Selma, Chicago, and other places as well. His ethic was tested by the cry for "Black Power!" which came primarily, though not exclusively, from a younger generation of civil rights activists, as well as by the controversy surrounding King's stand on the Vietnam war. These critical areas of conflict and growth helped King refine his nonviolent ethic methodologically, even as he was becoming personally more and more committed philosophically to nonviolence as a way of life.

The Albany Movement

In the fall of 1961 Charles Sherrod and Cordell Reagan, two workers of the Student Nonviolent Coordinating Committee (SNCC), arrived by bus in Albany, Georgia, to organize a voter registration campaign. Two months after their arrival Albany was the scene of the first large-scale uprising by a black community since the Montgomery bus boycott. The mass arrests made Albany a prototype for the campaigns that later rocked Birmingham and other cities throughout the nation. It also represented "a permanent turn from the lunch counter and the bus terminal to the streets, from hit-and-run attacks by students and professional civil rights workers to populist rebellion by lower-class [American blacks]."[4] The Albany movement grew out of the arrests of some freedom riders and the local college students who had attempted to integrate the bus terminal facilities in Albany. The local organization which was formed in response to those arrests was an amalgam of SNCC organizers, local college students, and leaders of Albany's established black civic and political organizations. When the local leaders officially invited King and his Southern Christian Leadership Conference (SCLC) team to Albany in December, more than five hundred protesters had already been arrested.

Upon arrival in Albany, King attempted to experiment with a new concept in the freedom struggle. He embarked upon an across-the-board, full-scale offensive against the system of segregation, per se, by bringing to bear upon the situation the full weight of the black community. In Albany his goal was not only the integrating of certain facilities and services but also the breaking of Albany's rigidly segregated lifestyle. His goal was for Albany to recognize its black community as a viable and significant political and economic entity that must be reckoned with and treated with respect, rather than be taken for granted. The city's uncompromising maintenance of its segregated institu-

tions and Police Chief Laurie Pritchett's gentlemanly handling
of the demonstrators in public made the Albany campaign a
difficult one to wage. In addition there were other problems
which beset the movement. To begin with, the decision to invite
King was not a unanimous one. Sherrod and Reagan, for example, were openly hostile. The SNCC leaders charged, pri-
vately at first and then publicly—as the movement dragged on
and their frustrations and annoyance increased—that time and
time again in one Southern community after another, SNCC did
the spadework and planted the seed, while King and the SCLC
reaped the harvest.

Some of the community leaders preferred to keep the focus,
goals, and leadership of the movement local. They had no desire
to see it become a rhetorically charged and grandly symbolic
struggle between the white and black South, nor a struggle between good and evil or the forces of light and the forces of
darkness. They believed that the local leaders, who must remain
after King and his lieutenants had gone back to Atlanta—King's
home at the time—and after the press had packed up and gone
home, should determine policy. The arrogance of some of the
SCLC staff persons and the way that they dealt with some of
the local people was also a source of conflict within the ranks of
the movement.

In addition to their internal problems, or perhaps partly because of them, the leaders of the Albany movement were unable
to capitalize on the errors made by the opposition in the three
arrests of Martin King during the course of the campaign. Westin
and Mahoney have stated that the jailings of King on such charges
as obstructing a sidewalk or parading without a permit provided
the movement with a much-needed cause around which national
pressure could be mounted against the city's public officials.
However, each time, just when it seemed that the city would
be forced to yield in its intransigence under the glare of national
publicity, something would happen to bring King out of jail:

> Once it was a promise by city officials (later rescinded) to open mean-
> ingful negotiations. Another time it was the need to get medical
> attention for one of the imprisoned local leaders who refused to leave
> jail as long as King remained behind bars. The third time an "anon-
> ymous" person paid King's fine in order to obtain his release. Each
> time he emerged from jail, the effect was to defuse the Movement

and lighten the pressure on the city.[5]

In 1962 a bus boycott was initiated and within three weeks the bus company, which depended heavily on the black community, halted its operations. Meanwhile, white businessmen, fearing a possible domino effect upon their enterprises, negotiated with representatives of the Albany movement to get the buses operating again and reached what was probably the first major desegregation agreement in Albany history—the resumption of bus service on an integrated basis. The acceptance of applications from blacks who sought jobs as drivers was also a significant part of the package. The city commission, however, refused to issue a written statement pledging noninterference with bus integration. The movement leaders decided not to accept the bus desegregation agreement without a written commitment from the city. The bus company, however, hired a black driver in the hope that the boycott would cease and reopened operations on a limited basis, but operations were ultimately forced to shut down. David Lewis has stated that because King was commuting between Atlanta and Albany, it was difficult for him at times to distinguish between the theoretical and the practical possibilities of the Albany situation.

> He was applying to it the lessons of Montgomery instead of revising his ideas in the light of the present circumstances. Instead of fighting for the written statement, it would have been better to have sent the black population en masse back to the buses to sit where it pleased.[6]

Thus, the movement failed to integrate the buses, and refusal to accept the negotiated settlement alienated the movement from the white business community and a number of white moderates who were sympathetic to the campaign. Again, the Albany leaders showed an inability to score a victory even when they had the opportunity to achieve one.

After eighteen months of mass meetings, demonstrations, and arrests, the city leaders were still adamant in their pro-segregationist stance; the lunch counters of the local department stores were still segregated; public facilities such as parks were either closed or had been sold to a group of Albany businessmen; no black policemen or bus drivers had been hired; and the plight of the black worker had not been upgraded.

King recognized that mistakes had been made and that the movement had failed to attain its goals. However, he also pointed out that setbacks were a part of any ongoing movement, especially when its tacticians were still experimenting and learning about their method of resistance. He further observed that no matter how sound a tactical theory of resistance happened to be, it still depended upon imperfect and frail human beings. It is they who constitute the mechanism to execute any social movement. He wrote: "They [human beings] must make mistakes and learn from them, make more mistakes and learn anew. They must taste defeat as well as success, and discover how to live with each. Time and action are the teachers."[7] Although King recognized the mistakes of the Albany movement, he refused to regard it as an unqualified failure. He noted that although lunch counters had remained segregated, blacks had begun registering to vote. The fact that the opponent had to cripple himself and his children by closing down such facilities as parks, libraries, and bus lines to obstruct the progress of blacks meant for King that the movement had been checked but not defeated. He was also encouraged by the response of Albany blacks to the appeal of nonviolence. He estimated that five percent of the total black community willingly went to jail and noted:

Were that percentage duplicated in New York City, some fifty thousand Negroes would overflow its prisons. If a people can produce from its ranks 5 per cent who will go voluntarily to jail for a just cause, surely nothing can thwart its ultimate triumph.[8]

If Montgomery gave King his first nonviolent victory and his initial experience in the use of the boycott as a form of nonviolent protest, it also gave him a rather simplistic and exaggerated conception of the power of nonviolence in and of itself. There was no real appreciation for and understanding of the other significant factors which added to the possibilities of its success. If King had given more serious thought and attention to such factors as timing, the methods of the opposition, and the courts, he might have been better prepared for Albany. Albany taught King that nonviolence, with its theological assumptions and ethical implications, was no irresistible force under which the walls of segregation would automatically crumble. If Montgomery demonstrated that when the timing and the incident were right, blacks could spontaneously organize themselves against racial injustice, then Albany taught King the importance of planning in sustaining a movement and carrying it through to victory. If Montgomery demonstrated that harsh repression by the adversary could generate sympathy and outside pressures on behalf of the victimized, then Albany taught King that an opponent who wears the facade of gentleness could halt the efforts of sympathetic outsiders and produce a sense of futility among the resisters. If Montgomery demonstrated that black unity could bring victory, then Albany taught King that disunity, distrust, and disagreement over matters of strategy could make a once vibrant movement lethargic. It could so disconcert its leaders that they would be unable to capitalize either on their gains or on the mistakes of their opposition. If Montgomery demonstrated that blacks could be mobilized around a single, clearly visible symbol or target of injustice, Albany taught King the tragedy of aiming at everything in general and nothing in particular. As the reservations of the black religious perspectives and the Christian realism of Reinhold Niebuhr were sobering influences upon the optimistic anthropological assumptions of evangelical liberalism for King, so Albany was a sobering influence upon the naiveté of his ethic of nonviolence regarding the power of his theological and moral assumptions, in and of themselves, to effect social change.

Albany was also significant because of the rifts that occurred between SCLC and two of its constituencies, during and subsequent to the campaign. One rift was internal, while the other was external. Before Albany, attempts had been made to keep within movement circles the differences of opinion between SCLC and SNCC regarding strategies, programs, and the nature of the commitment to nonviolence. SNCC was also dissatisfied with the treatment that it received from its parent body, the SCLC, and with King's leadership style. SNCC resented SCLC for preempting SNCC and assuming the leadership and receiving the glory from those campaigns whose groundwork had been done by SNCC. After Albany, the irreconcilable differences and disagreements between SCLC and SNCC were no longer secrets. The disagreements were no longer known only among those within or closely associated with the leadership strata of the civil rights movement. After Albany, the rift that occurred during the course of the campaign became more public and grew wider and deeper.

Prior to Albany, King and the SCLC had regarded the federal government and such enforcement agencies as the FBI as being among their strongest and most supportive allies. However, the failure of the federal government and the FBI to intervene or respond aggressively in behalf of Albany's blacks made the civil rights leadership aware that government could not be counted on, even at the federal level. The support needed to protect, enhance, and safeguard the rights and liberties of black Americans was not forthcoming. Although he continued to rely upon the backing and support of the federal government in other campaigns, its lethargic response in Albany caused King to view it more warily. His view was a more realistic one. After Albany, King became more critical of the FBI, and the rift that resulted from this criticism became a permanent, irreparable breach, the repercussions of which would be felt by King for the remainder of his life. Thus, Albany was a sobering experience for King in a number of ways.

Albany was one of the darkest hours in the early part of King's career as a social prophet and nonviolent practitioner. He would have many other dark hours in the years ahead and campaigns to come. After Montgomery, King's name became a household word; and prior to Albany his efforts had been crowned with success. The Albany failure, as failures always do, highlighted his vulnerabilities as a strategist and as a leader. Albany demonstrated that nonviolence was no invincible steamroller that insured success every time it was applied. Albany demonstrated that the success of nonviolence, or of any method of social protest and change, is dependent upon a number of other factors. However, if Albany was one of the darkest hours that King had faced thus far, then Birmingham provided the dawn.

Birmingham

The Albany defeat weighed heavily in the planning of the Birmingham campaign. King and SCLC attempted to make sure that the same tactical errors that cost them victory in Albany would not be repeated in Birmingham. To begin with, they made their goals more specific. Instead of attacking segregation on all fronts, they decided to concentrate on the business community. There were a number of advantages in concentrating on the business community. First, the buying power of the black community made the difference between profit and loss for a number of businessmen, some of whom were already hurting because of losses suffered during a prior boycott. Second, all the downtown stores were located in a relatively small, twelve-square-block business district where the demonstrations were bound to attract attention. Third, many of the merchants had already indicated that they would comply with the desegregation demands if permitted to do so by the city authorities. Fourth, since some of the stores were branches of nationwide companies (such as Woolworth's, W.L. Green's, and Newberry's), it was believed that pressure on national managements could be generated in the North. Fifth, it was also hoped that some of the merchants could be pressured to encourage others in the white community to begin negotiating with the blacks. Due to the special humiliation that black customers experienced in having their money accepted in every department in a store except the lunch counter, it was decided to target specifically those stores with lunch counters. The focus on the lunch counter added a symbolic dimension to the struggle and gave the effort a definite practical advantage. The lunch counter was a symbol with which every black shopper could identify. Thus, the movement increased its base of support by targeting a specific area of abuse, which generated broad appeal and receptivity in the black community.

The failure to identify a specific point of protest, the lack of detailed advanced planning, the element of timing, and the inability to achieve unity within the internal ranks of the movement were all factors that contributed to the failure of the Albany movement. King and his aides sought to correct these factors in their preparation for Birmingham.

King and his aides, in the tradition and style of Thoreauvian civil disobedience, also made an important philosophical and tactical decision on the issue of court injunctions that had challenged them before and that would haunt them even more poignantly after Birmingham. There were times when the civil rights movement had been the benefactor of injunctions. In 1961, for example, a federal court injunction was issued forbidding police officials and Klan groups from interfering with the freedom riders. However, as Lewis has observed, "Time—delays, legal feints, slow negotiations—was always the nonviolent movement's greatest foe."[9] Thus, the injunction process, working against rather than for the civil rights movement, was consistent historically with the way that it has functioned in the life of protest movements.

Historically, the injunction has been the instrument for the maintenance of the establishment rather than a means of protest by the oppressed. Dating from the 1890s when they had achieved widespread use by employers who sought to halt protest activities by labor unions, injunctions were frequently decisive in breaking strikes. Like the demonstrations that King was hoping to stage in Birmingham, the strike was generally the climax of a long and difficult planning process whose momentum built up gradually. Once the strike was halted, the momentum was often permanently lost. Although temporary injunctions were supposed to last for only a few days, it would often take weeks for hearings to be held leading to a continuation of the injunction until a full trial could decide whether or not the injunction should be made permanent. In the meantime, if the party against whom the injunction was issued violated any of its stipulations, that party would be subject to punishment for contempt of court.

The experience of the Albany campaign weighed heavily in the counsels of SCLC as King and his lieutenants wrestled with the injunction issue. During the Albany campaign a federal injunction had been issued restraining SCLC operations for ten days. King agreed to comply with the injunction while petitioning the U.S. Court of Appeals to overturn it. Although SCLC won this particular battle, it lost the war because the delay had damaged King's credibility in Albany's black community and among the SNCC organizers. "After they agreed to abide by the injunction, King and his aides were never able to assume effective leadership of the campaign, and factional quarrels grew in intensity. More demonstrations were held, but the civil rights forces could not bring city officials into meaningful negotiations."[10]

In explaining King's reticence to defy a federal injunction in Albany and how it affected him afterward, then SCLC staff member Andrew Young said that at the time of the Albany movement

King considered the federal courts as the only real national ally that the civil rights movement had. The federal courts had challenged segregation in travel, in public accommodations, and with the 1954 school desegregation order, they had challenged discrimination in education. They had also assisted in Montgomery. The defiance, then, of their injunction in Albany would have been a slap in the face of the federal courts, something that King could not bring himself to do. After the Albany campaign collapsed, however, King regretted his decision to obey the injunction. Consequently, he entered the planning for Birmingham ready to defy even a federal court injunction rather than see a repeat of Albany. He believed that if he were to allow the movement to be stopped by an injunction in Birmingham, then the same technique would be used against the movement everywhere throughout the South.

King identified the injunction process as the South's leading instrument in blocking the "direct action civil rights movement" and in preventing blacks and whites from engaging in peaceful protests, which were rights guaranteed by the First Amendment. In describing how injunctions had been used against the movement and his decision to defy those issued against him in Birmingham, he wrote:

> You initiate a nonviolent demonstration. The power structure secures an injunction against you. It can conceivably take two or three years before any disposition of the case is made. The Alabama courts are notorious for "sitting on" cases of this nature. This has been a maliciously effective, pseudo-legal way of breaking the back of legitimate moral protest.
>
> We had anticipated that the procedure would be used in Birmingham. It had been invoked in Montgomery to outlaw our car pool during the bus boycott. It had destroyed the protest movement in Talladega, Alabama. It had torpedoed our effort in Albany, Georgia. It had routed the N.A.A.C.P. from the state of Alabama. We decided, therefore, knowing well what the consequences would be and prepared to accept them, that we had no choice but to violate such an injunction. [11]

On Wednesday, April 3, 1963, after months of planning, King opened the Birmingham campaign with the announcement that he would lead demonstrations there until "Pharaoh lets God's people go." Another lesson that King had learned in Albany and in other campaigns was that a mass movement had to be built to a climax and that a loss of momentum was fatal. Consequently, the campaign started slowly with scouting operations such as token sit-ins and small demonstrations designed primarily to probe the opposition and attract the attention of the black community. King's participation in these opening maneuvers was minimal. His time was spent placating the sensitivities and gaining the support of the city's local black leaders, many of whom were opposed to the campaign. Due to a tense mayoralty struggle between the die-hard segregationist Bull Connor and the moderate segregationist Albert Boutwell, King felt that it was strategically necessary to plan for the Birmingham campaign (code named "Project C") with a degree of secrecy to prevent the Connor forces from capitalizing on the upcoming demonstrations. Secret planning, however, shut out not only the opponent but also the leadership of the black community. Consequently there were blacks who resented not being informed of the campaign's starting date or of its plan of operation. They resented being pulled into a movement that they had no part in organizing and into which they had given no input. However, with every argument and verbal resource at his command, King managed to explain, cajole, preach, and pressure most of the black leadership into supporting the movement.

With his base in the black community secured, King opened Phase II of Project C on April 6, 1963, with a token street demonstration. The next day, which was Palm Sunday, the first incident of conflict occurred between the demonstrators and the police. During the first three days of demonstrations Bull Connor, behaving like the comparatively benign Laurie Pritchett of Albany, had been unusually mild in his handling of the protesters. Possibly the tactic of gently handling protesters in public could have worked in Birmingham as it had done in Albany. However, Connor was a man of little patience and was not really committed to the nonviolent treatment of demonstrators. His forbearance was contingent upon his expectation that a forthcoming injunction would end the demonstrations. That injunction was delivered to King on April 10, and two days later, on Good Friday, King followed through on his earlier resolve and marched in defiance of the injunction.

The arrest of King and his lieutenants as they marched in defiance of the injunction was an important turning point in the campaign. It was a turning point in terms of Connor's handling of the protesters. Since the injunction had failed to halt the demonstrations, Connor began to resort to violence. It was also a turning point in terms of public opinion, which began to shift in support of the Birmingham demonstrations. This shift of public opinion was given impetus by King's famous "Letter from a Birmingham Jail," which he wrote during his confinement as a response to a public letter from eight of the city's leading white clergymen in which they criticized King and the campaign and appealed to the black community to withdraw its support. Four days later, after finishing the letter, King sensing that the campaign needed his presence, posted bond and resumed personal leadership of the movement.

With King at the helm of the movement, it was decided to initiate Phase III, which called for the involvement of Birmingham's young people in the campaign. Earlier in the campaign, while King was answering his critics and garnering support from the black community, SCLC staff member James Bevel had been involved in an activity which would later prove to be the most controversial aspect of the Birmingham strategy. Bevel had begun to organize high school and grammar school children. This tactic had already been used in Statesville and Durham, North Carolina. Children had also been used in Albany under different circumstances. In other SCLC-sponsored direct-action crusades, the young people had been the prime movers. In Birmingham, however, two-thirds of those arrested had been adults. With adult enthusiasm and participation waning, with an impasse reached in the negotiations with city officials, it was felt that the time had come to enlist the youth in larger numbers. Although King knew that he would be criticized severely for using children, he felt the movement needed this "dramatic new dimension." Like all of the other major decisions involved in the Birmingham campaign, this one was not reached easily. Bennett has written:

> It is easy, in retrospect, to say that the decision they made was brilliant. But the sun was hooded by clouds then and few men were willing to assume the awesome responsibility for the possible death of a child. Many men said later that they made the big decision. But back there, it was all in one man's hands, and history will note that sometime before May 2, 1963, Martin Luther King, Jr. gave his assent

to one of the most momentous decisions in the history of Negro protests. In that hour, eyes red from lack of sleep, he took upon his shoulders the awful burden of committing thousands of children to the front lines of a battle that was being fought (by policemen and firemen) with billy clubs, fierce dogs and water hoses that could strip bark from an oak tree.[12]

Thursday, May 2, was the day that the black elementary and secondary school students of Birmingham began their assault on the city's system of segregation. On that day approximately one thousand of them were arrested, with violence kept to a minimum. On the next day, however, when an even larger crowd of young people turned out, Bull Connor made a fateful decision which would turn the tide of public opinion against him. He decided to use dogs and water hoses to prevent the demonstrators from reaching the downtown area. The brutality of Connor's counterattack, the sight of policemen, with sticks and dogs, wading into crowds, coupled with the sight of children being knocked over with high-pressure water hoses, angered adult bystanders who responded by throwing bricks and bottles. Photographs of police dogs biting black children circled the globe, revolting millions and changing public sentiment almost overnight.

King made it clear that he had no intention of relaxing pressure. Unlike the Albany situation in which he showed an inability to take advantage of whatever gains came to the movement, King in Birmingham was determined to capitalize on the tactical errors of the opponents. He said in the midst of the daily escalating crisis: "We are ready to negotiate . . . But we intend to negotiate from strength. If the white power structure of this city will meet some of our minimum demands, then we will consider calling off the demonstrations, but we want promises, plus action."[13]

With Birmingham teetering at the precipice of civic and social collapse, being strained to the breaking point, with black patience growing thin as Connor became more brutal and repressive in his tactics, and with the direct effect the demonstrations were having upon the economic life of the downtown shopping area, negotiations began between leaders of Birmingham's white community and SCLC. On May 10 King announced that an agreement had been reached which consisted of four pledges:

1. The desegregation of lunch counters, rest rooms, fitting rooms and drinking fountains, in planned stages within ninety days after signing.

2. The upgrading and hiring of Negroes on a nondiscriminatory basis throughout the industrial community of Birmingham, to include hiring of Negroes as clerks and salesmen within sixty days after signing of the agreement—and the immediate appointment of a committee of business, industrial and professional leaders to implement an area-wide program for the acceleration of upgrading and employment of Negroes in job categories previously denied to them.

3. Official cooperation with the movement's legal representatives in working out the release of all jailed persons on bond or on their personal recognizance.

4. Through the Senior Citizens Committee or Chamber of Commerce, communications between Negro and white to be publicly established within two weeks after signing, in order to prevent the necessity of further demonstrations and protests. [14]

Birmingham racists responded to the agreement by bombing the home of A.D. King (Martin's brother) and the Gaston Motel (which had served as SCLC headquarters). Birmingham blacks responded to the bombings by rioting. However, after moderate voices in the white community began condemning the violence and calling for order, Birmingham settled down to an uneasy peace.

The sobering influence of Albany upon King was reflected in the planning for both the Birmingham and the Selma campaigns. In both of these campaigns King strategized the application of his nonviolent ethic with a fastidiousness that was not evident before Albany. Careful attention was given to such particulars as the selection of a goal that was specific enough to be clearly delineated and attainable, yet broad enough to have unifying potential. The implications of public opinion for the campaign's success or failure and the extent to which federal and economic pressures could be generated to impact the local situation were also considered. The likelihood of the opponent to overreact against the demonstrators with excessive violence was another factor in the planning. The strategies of his campaigns showed that nonviolence, as used by King, was not only coercive but also manipulative. Although the ideals and the rhetoric of the principles of nonviolence were still adhered to, after Albany King began to pay more attention to the practical aspects of nonviolence (i.e., what actually worked to achieve the specific goals of the campaign).

Love was not given the emphasis in the rhetoric of the Birmingham campaign that it received during the Montgomery bus boycott. The rhetoric of Birmingham reflected the temper of the times within the movement. By the time the Birmingham campaign occurred, the restless student element that was always a potential "Achilles heel" for King's philosophy and style of leadership, had begun to wrestle with the nature of its commitment to nonviolence. Instead of a moral commitment, the students made only a tactical commitment to nonviolence. In their approach to nonviolence, for love to be the heart of the nonviolent method was a non sequitur.

Although the theme of love was not at the center of the movement, nor as much a part of King's rhetoric during and after Birmingham as it had been during the Montgomery bus boycott, love nevertheless remained at the heart of King's personal philosophy and ethic. His personal commitment to love as the vital center for the most effective application of nonviolence, both as a method and as a philosophy of life, remained throughout the rest of his life.

The Birmingham campaign was significant in the development of King's ethic from a practical standpoint. It was the laboratory in which King tested the lessons gleaned from the Albany movement. It was also significant for the civil rights movement as a whole. The student element within the movement was not the only part of King's constituency that began to waver in its philosophical commitment to nonviolence. The members of the Kennedy administration and Northern whites were not the only persons to view defenseless, black school children being knocked off their feet by high-pressure water hoses. Black people also observed the inhumane treatment of their racial kin. The brutal treatment of blacks by the Birmingham police and the bombing of Sixteenth Street Baptist Church was the proverbial "last straw" for a number of blacks in terms of their commitment to nonviolence as a philosophy. As more and more blacks raised questions about nonviolence, a new intensity and impatience became evident in black demands. After Birmingham, the movement that had been basically Southern moved north, and the major urban centers of the North found themselves embroiled in the surging tide of black dissatisfaction and the quest of black America for true equality.

The new intensity was not brought on only by the increasing number of blacks who began to raise questions about the efficacy of nonviolence, both as a philosophy and as a tactic. It was also augmented by King's defiance of the Birmingham injunction. As the courts increasingly issued injunctions against demonstrations, various groups of protesters became bolder in defying injunctions in the name of the higher cause of justice. These groups used King's arguments that the voluntary submission to the punishment resulting from their defiance was a hedge against anarchy and that such submission demonstrated the resisters' basic respect for the law.

The civil rights movement reached its zenith after Birmingham. Concern for the civil rights of black Americans became a priority in the national consciousness as it has not been in this century, either before or since Birmingham. Thus, Birmingham was more than the dawn needed after the dark night of Albany. It was actually the high noon of King's career and of the civil rights movement.

Selma

At the beginning of 1965, the need for federal legislation to protect the voting rights of black Americans had become the top priority of King and other civil rights leaders. Selma, Alabama, became the target community that King would use to mobilize national opinion on the voting rights issue. Selma was to be one of King's most interesting campaigns in that it bore similarities to both the Albany and the Birmingham campaigns. In Selma, King would face Wilson Baker, the public safety director, whose philosophy and style of law enforcement were similar to those of Albany's police chief Laurie Pritchett. More important for the successful implementation of the SCLC strategy of nonviolent protest in Selma, King would also face Sheriff James ("Jim") Clark of Dallas County. Wilson Baker was the chief law enforcement officer within the town of Selma. Jim Clark was the chief law enforcement officer of Dallas County, Alabama, whose government seat was Selma. Baker claimed jurisdiction over law enforcement within the city limits. Clark claimed jurisdiction over the county courthouse, located within the city limits, which was the focal point of the demonstrations. All during the Selma campaign the relationship between Clark and Baker was strained at best, and there were times when the conflict between the two of them seemed to be just as intense as it was between them and the demonstrators. Jim Clark, like Birmingham's Bull Connor, was an important factor in determining SCLC's strategy for the Selma campaign.

The dramatic failure in Albany and the qualified victory in Birmingham indicated to King and his staff that white violence, which was seen as unprovoked, was to the movement's advantage. National attention heightened and public opinion shifted quickly in favor of the protesters' cause when white lawmen used tactics such as Connor's against demonstrators. Consequently, it was theorized that one of the most effective stimulants for a heightened national interest in new voting rights legislation would be white violence used against blacks who were peacefully seeking to register and vote. The choice of Selma for the 1965 SCLC voting rights campaign partly grew out of this tactical consideration. Clark's repression of the SNCC voter education and registration efforts in Dallas County seemed to indicate that he was likely to lose his temper and respond violently when confronted with determined demonstrators. If the demonstrations could evoke from Clark a public violent response like Connor's rather than a private violent response like Pritchett's, then the SCLC effort to focus national attention on the need for stronger voting rights legislation to protect black Americans, who were attempting to exercise a constitutional right, would be greatly augmented.

On Monday, January 18, 1965, King led his first march in the Selma campaign to the Dallas County Courthouse. It was also a crucial day from Wilson Baker's perspective. Baker knew that part of King's strategy called for demonstrations in several other "black belt" counties. If Selma did not provide the needed action, then King would leave a token force in Dallas County and shift the main contingent of the campaign, along with its publicity, to wherever the most visible opposition developed. Consequently, it was imperative from Baker's point of view that the activities on January 18 remain peaceful, especially at the courthouse. After some intense negotiations, Clark reluctantly assented to

Baker's viewpoint. Thus, the first day of demonstrations went by without an incident of violence.

Baker's success in keeping the day's events and Sheriff Clark under control was discussed extensively at an SCLC staff meeting that night. Baker had even quietly arrested the American Nazi Party leader George Lincoln Rockwell to prevent him from entering a mass meeting at Brown's Chapel AME Church where he had planned to speak. SCLC knew that without some action, the press would not stay around to give the movement the kind of national exposure that it needed. It was decided that another march would be attempted the next day, January 19, and if the events lacked the drama needed to make the campaign newsworthy, then SCLC would begin shifting its activities to other black belt counties. Such a change of plans, however, would not be necessary—Jim Clark would see to that.

On January 19, when the marchers arrived at the courthouse and told Clark that they were going to enter the front door and were not going into any alley, he immediately began arresting them. One of the first persons he grabbed was Mrs. Amelia Boynton, a well-known local leader. When she didn't move fast enough to please him, Clark grabbed her by the back of the collar and in full view of the reporters and other marchers, pushed her stumbling halfway down the block to a sheriff's car. This was the kind of treatment that the SCLC had expected from Clark. At a mass meeting that night King's closest companion and aide, the Reverend Ralph Abernathy, wryly proposed that the Dallas County Voters' League accept Jim Clark into honorary membership for his "sterling service in bringing the plight of black people in Selma to the attention of the nation."[15]

The Selma campaign proceeded with mounting tension between the King-led demonstrators and the Clark-led forces. There was also an ever-widening gap between Wilson Baker and Jim Clark over the latter's handling of demonstrators. Like King's previous campaigns, Selma had its significant events—its high as well as its low moments. One of those high events was a protest march which was led by local black public school teachers. The teachers' march was meaningful not only for the local people of Selma but also for the SCLC and SNCC workers who had come from other parts of the South. Black educators had been viewed by SCLC and SNCC as the most reticent of all the leadership groups in the black community. A number of the movement's staff persons had become full-time civil rights workers after being expelled from Southern high schools and colleges by fearful, compromised black administrators. They had also been put out of school after school and tossed off campus after campus across the South as they sought to recruit black students for the movement. Thus, the march by the teachers signified to the SNCC and SCLC staff that the voting rights campaign had truly "come of age." It had developed its own spirit and momentum among Selma's blacks as they, of their own accord— as a total community—affirmed and legitimated the struggle.

Another event of significance occurred on Thursday, February 4, when SCLC staff persons were startled by the unannounced arrival of the articulate former Black Muslim leader Malcolm X. Malcolm X had been invited to Selma by some SNCC people who had gone to Tuskegee, Alabama, the night before to hear him speak. Malcolm X had been very critical of nonviolence and the goals and leadership of the civil rights movement. In his speech "Message to the Grass Roots" he had said:

> You don't have a turn-the-other-cheek revolution. There's no such thing as a nonviolent revolution. . . . The only revolution in which the goal is loving your enemy is the Negro revolution. It's the only revolution in which the goal is a desegregated lunch counter, a desegregated theater, a desegregated park, and a desegregated public toilet; you can sit down next to white folks—on the toilet. That's no revolution. . . . Whoever heard of a revolution where they lock arms . . . singing "We Shall Overcome"? You don't do that in a revolution. You don't do any singing, you're too busy swinging.[16]

The SCLC staff members were aware of Malcolm X's view about nonviolence. They also knew that he was very popular among a number of blacks, especially the young people. Consequently, they were skeptical about giving him an opportunity to speak, fearing that his oratory might leave the SCLC staff with a situation that they could not control. The SNCC people, however, were so adamant in their insistence that he be allowed to speak to the several hundred persons, who were mostly young and who had gathered at Brown's Chapel AME Church to receive the day's instructions and marching orders, that the SCLC staff reluctantly assented to the SNCC leaders' demands. Martin Luther King was not present because he was in jail at the time.

Malcolm X, however, was restrained in his remarks. He said that the whites should be thankful for Dr. King since there were those who didn't believe in his methods. He urged his listeners to present their case to the White House by reminding President Johnson that 97 percent of the black vote had gone to him. If the White House was unresponsive, he then urged blacks to take their concerns to the United Nations and place racism in America on trial before the world.

After speaking, Malcolm X was introduced to Mrs. Coretta King, who had arrived as he was finishing his speech. Malcolm X assured Mrs. King that he hadn't come to Selma to make her husband's job more difficult but, he hoped, to make it easier. If whites realized what the alternative was, then perhaps they would be more willing to listen to Dr. King. He also stated that he had wanted to visit Dr. King in jail but would be unable to do so because he had to catch a plane to London where he was to address the African Student Congress. Mrs. King was impressed with Malcolm X's sincerity and gave his message to her husband when she saw him later that day. This incident proved to be his last opportunity to meet with King, because in less than three weeks Malcolm X was gunned down in Harlem.

However, if there was a single event or march or day that made the Selma campaign successful, it was the march of Sunday, March 7, 1965. On that day approximately six hundred marchers, led by Hosea Williams of SCLC and John Lewis of SNCC, were teargassed, cattle prodded, and beaten with such a degree of barbarism that after the melee more than seventeen blacks had to be hospitalized and fifty to sixty others had to be given some kind of emergency medical treatment. Words cannot adequately explain the horror that many Americans felt as they watched on their televisions the attack of posse members and state troopers upon the demonstrators. Jim Clark and Colonel Al Lingo, Clark's personal friend and commander of the contingent of the Alabama State Police sent to Selma to maintain order, were responsible for the attack on the marchers. As Bull Connor's use of dogs and water hoses irrevocably shifted the weight of public opinion to the Birmingham blacks, Clark and Lingo's excessive use of force in turning back the marchers on the Pettus Bridge had the same effect on the Selma campaign.

King, in response to the events of "Bloody Sunday," sent

telegrams to about two hundred religious leaders asking them to join him in Selma for a ministers' march to Montgomery to take place on Tuesday, March 9. On Monday, March 8, SCLC lawyers went to the federal district court in Montgomery to secure an injunction to prevent Alabama Governor George Wallace, Lingo, and Clark from interfering with the right of the protesters to march and to ask for the protection of the protesters as they marched. By naming Wallace as a defendant and filing the suit in Montgomery, the SCLC lawyers were able to keep the case out of the lower courts that were sympathetic to the defendants. Instead the case was heard by a highly respected federal judge, who had a commendable record on civil rights: Judge Frank Johnson, who presided over the district in which Montgomery was located.

Presenting the case before Johnson, from the standpoint of the SCLC lawyers, seemed like a shrewd tactical move. However, it quickly had the opposite effect. Judge Johnson, noting that some of the defendants had not been notified of the application, denied the request of an immediate restraining order and set Thursday, March 11, as the date for a full hearing. He also enjoined any further demonstrations until after the Thursday hearing could be held, precluding King's march planned for Tuesday, March 9. Thus was created King's most acute and famous dilemma over the question of obedience to court orders. Although King had entered the Selma and Birmingham campaigns with a predetermined resolve to defy a court injunction which might cripple the movement, he possessed no "rule of thumb" concerning injunctions per se. His response to injunctions evolved out of the local situation. King's dilemma with the injunction issue has been described thus:

> In the South, which was still King's main theater of operations, the help of the courts (especially federal courts) was badly needed to spur compliance with desegregation, and King could not afford to lay himself open repeatedly to charges of violating a court order. It was one thing to proclaim defiance of a state court injunction in Birmingham, where SCLC itself had made a major commitment of time, resources, and prestige. When local civil rights leaders sought his aid in battles of their own, and it was not a major SCLC effort, King walked a careful line on the injunction issue. . . . It was in Selma that King would be put to his most painful personal test on the issue of how to respond to a court injunction.[17]

The dilemma for King was a crucial one; the consequences were portentous. There was a mood at the King headquarters which demanded action. There was a feeling that without a march or some kind of nonviolent response to the outrageous brutality on the Pettus Bridge, violence would surely erupt. In a religious movement in which confronting wrong was considered to be absolutely essential, one simply could not allow certain acts of injustice to occur without a response. King was also feeling the pressure to march from the more militant elements within the movement. In addition to these other factors, there was also the consideration of the numbers of clergymen and concerned black and white citizens who, in response to his "Macedonian call," were pouring into Selma from all parts of the country and who were psychologically prepared to march. Any postponement of the scheduled demonstration might produce a collapse in the movement's momentum like the one experienced in Albany three years earlier.

On the other hand, the federal court had been not only the movement's refuge in the midst of Southern inequities but also one of its strongest and most powerful supporters. Judge Johnson's record in the protection of civil rights in the federal judiciary was one of the best, South or North. President Lyndon B. Johnson had also contacted King on Monday, even before the injunction was issued, and asked him not to march. King either had to yield to the pressures from within himself and his constituency or had to march in violation of the injunction and strain severely, if not rupture altogether, the existing helpful relations between himself and the Johnson administration.

King met with his staff—James Farmer of the Congress of Racial Equality (CORE) and Jim Forman of SNCC—to discuss the pros and cons of proceeding with the scheduled march. According to Jim Forman, with the exception of Hosea Williams, the SCLC staff was in favor of postponing the march. Forman's position was that the judge's offer was legal blackmail since there was no guarantee of getting the injunction and no deadline for the completion of hearings on it. The consensus of the group, though, was to postpone the march. However, when King reached the church and saw the tremendous numbers of people who had responded to his call, he announced that the march would begin the next morning. After the mass meeting SCLC and SNCC staff persons held another strategy session to reconsider the decision to march. After three hours it was decided to proceed with the march. King then called U.S. Attorney General Nicholas Katzenbach and told him of the decision.

Upon learning of King's latest decision, the White House sent the head of the Community Relations Service (CRS), former Florida Governor Leroy Collins, by government jet to Selma. Mr. Collins met with King early Tuesday morning to persuade him to change his mind. Failing to persuade King, Collins then met secretly with Clark and Lingo, who agreed not to attack the marchers if they stopped when ordered to do so and returned to the church. There is some uncertainty as to whether or not King agreed to this plan. [18]

As the march started, Collins rushed up to King and told him that he felt that everything would be all right and handed him a small piece of paper, which King assumed contained the route that Wilson Baker wanted the march to follow. It was the same route that the march had followed the previous Sunday. The march, made up of more than three thousand persons, proceeded to cross the Pettus Bridge until ordered to halt by Major John Cloud, who along with the troopers, was stationed on the other side. King asked for permission to pray. It was granted. Immediately after the prayer Major Cloud abruptly turned and ordered the troopers to clear the road, leaving the highway to Montgomery open to the marchers. King, however, directed the line to proceed back to Brown's Chapel AME Church.

The action King took on the Pettus Bridge did irreparable damage to the already strained relationships that existed between SCLC and SNCC. Although it had been rumored, and some persons had suspected, that King would turn back, there were many others, among them Jim Forman and other SNCC people, who knew nothing of any agreement and who felt dismayed, baffled, and angry when the march was turned around. Later that day, King issued a ban on all marches in Selma and Montgomery pending the outcome of the injunction suit. However, on the next day SNCC proceeded to hold a march in Montgomery at the capitol, which had already been planned with students from Tuskegee Institute.

While SNCC-directed students were demonstrating in Montgomery, the demonstrators in Selma were participating in a prayer vigil for the recovery of the Reverend James Reeb, a white Unitarian minister, who had been attacked by several white men and who would become the campaign's second fatality. (Jimmy Lee Jackson, a black person, had also been killed.) During this same period, the relationship between Clark and Baker became so strained that after having come to blows and threatening to kill each other, they started communicating through intermediaries. On Saturday, March 13, Governor Wallace flew to Washington to meet with President Johnson in a futile attempt to persuade the national administration to soften its stand on voting rights. On Monday, March 15, President Johnson delivered a strong address during which he announced that a voting rights bill would be sent to Congress by the next Wednesday. On March 19, Judge Johnson lifted his injunction against the march and directed the governor to give affirmative protection to the marchers. When Governor Wallace complained to the president that the state could not afford the burdensome expense involved in protecting the marchers, President Johnson used his powers to federalize the Alabama national guard, augmenting them with U.S. Army troops, U.S. marshals, and FBI agents. On Thursday, March 25, King led a throng of some 25,000 marchers to the federal building in Montgomery. The rally ended with a stirring speech by King.

That night, however, before the success of the march could be celebrated, white racists struck again. Mrs. Viola Liuzzo, a white woman from Detroit, became the third fatality of the Selma campaign.

On Friday, August 6, President Johnson signed into law the Voting Rights Act of 1965, which guaranteed the right to vote, created federal authority to register voters in areas and instances where local officials obstructed and interfered with registration procedures, and restricted the use of discriminatory examinations of potential voters.

Selma, like Birmingham, didn't just happen. There were any number of places which were just as guilty of denying the rights and suppressing the civil liberties of America's blacks as was Dallas County, Alabama. Selma was chosen because there were factors in the local situation, such as an ill-tempered and hostile sheriff, which could be manipulated and exploited to the advantages of the campaign and nonviolent victory. Selma was also an extension of Birmingham in terms of the injunction issue. The same philosophical arguments that King used to justify his decision that he would disobey any court injunction which could adversely affect the Birmingham movement were applicable to Selma. His decision not to march beyond the Pettus Bridge and his admission that he never intended to defy Judge Johnson's order indicate that at that point in his life King still cherished his relationship with the Johnson administration and was not prepared either to offend the White House or to defy the federal judiciary.

Selma was also an extension of Birmingham in terms of its goals. The goals of the Birmingham campaign were basically local with national implications. The goals of the Selma campaign were basically national in character with local implications. If there had been no federal legislation following the Birmingham campaign, King could have been satisfied with the local settlement. The local settlement would have been sufficient to restore confidence in the effectiveness of nonviolence and recoup the prestige that King lost through the failure of the Albany movement. In the 1965 campaign, on the other hand, King did not make allowance for a victory apart from new federal voting legislation. Although King always viewed his actions in the local situation in relationship to their broader implications for the whole of America, both black and white, his endeavors to influence the macrocosm were usually indirect or by inference and implication. In Selma, King directly engaged a major national issue and sought to influence the executive and legislative branches of the federal government. The significance of the Selma campaign in the development of King's nonviolent ethic can be seen partly in this effort to use nonviolence as more than a technique for the solution of local problems in the local community, that is, as a mechanism for change on the national level.

Selma was also a significant turning point for King and for the civil rights movement. Montgomery unlocked the doors of pride and self-confidence and of political and economic respect for the black community. Birmingham unlocked the doors of public accommodation to black people. Selma unlocked the doors of political access to Southern blacks. After all these doors had been opened, however, King and others who had been in the vanguard of the civil rights movement discovered that the masses of black people had been so maimed by an economic system that was both unjust and racist that they were unable to walk through the doors that had been opened. King discovered that although his civil rights gains were important and necessary victories for black Americans, these newly acquired freedoms did not touch black people where the hurt was greatest and deepest. Consequently, after Selma, King began to stress enabling black people to walk through the newly opened doors of opportunity as well as enhancing their access to these doors. In other words, he began to talk about economic justice.

When King became involved in the struggle for economic justice, he made several important discoveries. He discovered that economic justice is a much more complex and costlier issue than civil rights. He discovered that blacks were not the only persons who had been victimized economically in this society. In matters of economic inequity and injustice, blacks were surrounded by a "great multitude of witnesses." King also discovered that economic justice could not become a reality when the resources and priorities of this country were committed to a war in Southeast Asia. After Selma, then, King expanded his vision to include more than those concerns that could be isolated and characterized as "Southern" or "black" problems. His ethic went beyond region and race and became national in its thrust and international in its scope.

Selma, then, was a turning point for Martin Luther King, Jr., and the civil rights movement. Lewis has said:

> Those who listened carefully to his speeches after Montgomery— their tone as well as their content—realized that the imminent passage of a voting law would begin to close the books on Martin Luther King's role as an internationally acclaimed combatant for the rights solely of Southern blacks.[19]

Fager has also observed:

> There are other stories that could be told of Selma 1965. One of them is how the Southern civil rights movement of the decade came to an end there, with only the splendor of the march to Montgomery's success preventing the fact of its finality becoming immediately apparent to all.[20]

Louis Lomax has also identified the Selma-Montgomery march as the end of the nonviolent civil rights era which had begun in Montgomery ten years earlier and had catapulted King into national prominence. According to Lomax two things had happened. First, blacks had grown tired of being beaten and jailed for attempting to exercise their constitutional rights. Second, the gains of the civil rights movement had failed to sift down to the black masses, particularly in the Northern ghettoes of America.[21] It was to those black masses that King would next turn his attention.

4

The Maturing Ethic: Economic Justice and International Peace

Martin Luther King, Jr., like many of those who wrote about him, felt that the Selma campaign and the Voting Rights Act marked the end of one phase of the civil rights movement. At the time, however, not everyone was aware of the changes in emphasis and direction which were occurring within the movement. Consequently, a number of white Americans who had supported the aspirations of American blacks during the previous decades were unprepared for the demands and the implications of the second phase of the movement. In King's view the first phase of the movement had been a struggle to treat blacks with a degree of decency, which the vast majority of white Americans were willing to do. The second phase of the struggle, however, was an attempt to implement the legislative gains of the previous decade, taking seriously the verbal commitments of the president, the white press, and the pulpit to freedom, justice, and equality. White America, though willing to treat blacks with decency, was unprepared and unwilling to treat them equally. And when the equality mentality of phase-two blacks met the decency-but-not-equality mentality of phase-one whites, the result was havoc.

Blacks felt betrayed and cheated while whites felt that blacks, in the light of their recent gains, were pushing too fast, too hard, and for too much.

Much of the equality sought in phase two was expressed in terms of economic justice. King felt that white America was unprepared for the cost of economic justice. He felt that the reforms of the previous decades had been obtained at "bargain rates." It was not necessary to rewrite this nation's economic agenda or initiate any new tax reforms to integrate lunch counters, libraries, parks, and hotels. When integration became inescapable, it was discovered that even the psychological adjustment was far from formidable. White Southerners may have trembled under the strain, but they did not collapse. Even the more significant changes resulting from the voting rights struggle required neither great monetary nor psychological sacrifices. The real cost of achieving true equality, both in terms of psychological adjustment and the commitment of the fiscal resources of the nation, had yet to be paid. King felt that the stiffening of white resistance was a recognition of that fact. Thus he wrote:

> The paths of Negro-white unity that had been converging crossed at Selma, and like a giant X began to diverge. Up to Selma there had been unity to eliminate barbaric conduct. Beyond it the unity had to be based on the fulfillment of equality, and in the absence of agreement the paths began inexorably to move apart.[1]

After Selma, King not only found a lack of support among liberal whites who had previously supported him but also a belief that blacks, with federal help, were moving too rapidly. He was also faced with growing criticism in the black community. The black community's criticism essentially revolved around three concerns. First, as whites withdrew their support, blacks intensified their demands; or as blacks intensified their demands, whites withdrew their support. Either way, the fact remained that the black community became more militant. This militant mood, which especially gripped young blacks, ranged from impatience on the part of some toward nonviolence, both as a philosophy of life and as a method of protest, to open hostility and rejection by others who felt that it had accomplished too little too late too slowly.

Second, there was a feeling among a number of blacks, particularly young blacks, that the movement was being subtly manipulated by some of its powerful white allies and that some of its potential independence was being thwarted by the whites who were actively involved with it.

Third, blacks living in the large Northern urban areas were also disaffected by the nonviolent movement. The civil rights movement had produced little or no change in the quality of their lives.

In an interview, King admitted the failure of the nonviolent movement to alter radically the life of the Northern black when he said:

> Though many would prefer not to, we must face the fact that progress for the Negro—to which white "moderates" like to point in justifying gradualism—has been relatively insignificant, particularly in terms of the Negro masses. What little progress has been made—and that includes the Civil Rights Act—has applied primarily to the middle-class Negro. Among the masses, especially in the Northern ghettoes, the situation remains the same, and for some it's worse.[2]

This lack of progress for Northern blacks, in the opinion of King, accounted for the reason that there were more riots in the North than in the South. The Southern black could see some visible, concrete civil rights victories. The Harlem black, however, could see no victories. It was a sad commentary on the era of nonviolent protest that ended at Selma, and one of the greatest ironies of the entire civil rights movement, that less than one week after President Johnson signed into law the Voting Rights Act of 1965—amid glowing predictions that the black American was standing on a new threshold and amid the aura of what was considered a stunning victory for King and a shattering defeat for the forces of segregation—blacks rioted in the Watts ghetto of Los Angeles.

King was interested in a number of economic reforms, such as a guaranteed income for the poor, jobs, and massive federal programs for the enhancement of deprived communities. The application of his nonviolent ethic to economic justice, in the Chicago movement, was his only local campaign devoted exclusively to an aspect of economic justice (housing) rather than to civil rights.

The Chicago Campaign

In January 1966, King and his wife moved to Chicago (their children joined them later). In order to identify with the urban black poor that he was trying to help, King moved into an old tenement in a section of the ghetto known as Lawndale. King, to avoid receiving special treatment, did not rent the apartment in his own name. The apartment was leased by his aide Bernard Lee. The landlord, however, discovered who the real occupants would be and hastily had the apartment repainted, fumigated, and the heating system repaired. Even with the fresh paint and repairs, the apartment left much to be desired. It was located on the third floor of a dingy building with hallways that had no lights, dirty floors, and an overpowering smell of urine.

King met with Mayor Richard Daley, who assured him that all of the city's departments had been ordered to cooperate, and held another meeting with the chief of police. Certain that all bases had been touched, King announced the goals of the campaign. They were the education of the people about slum conditions, the organization of slum dwellers into a union to force landlords to fulfill their obligations to their tenants, and the mobilization of slum tenants into an army of nonviolent demonstrators. He also stated that he was prepared to engage in acts of civil disobedience to draw attention to a specific problem and to break laws to obey a higher law of humanity and justice.

During the month of February King announced that he had assumed "trusteeship" of a slum tenement, stating that he would have responsibility for the collection of rents and then use the money to clean and renovate the building. He referred to his move as "supralegal," asserting that the moral question was more important than the legal one. The city's response to King's move was an announcement that it had almost completed a dossier on the landlord which would lead to a court investigation. It felt that the question of the legality of the trusteeship was a private matter between the concerned parties. Meanwhile, the landlord offered to give King the building if he would take over the mortgage, but King refused. Although the trusteeship move received a great deal of publicity, it accomplished very little. In terms of public sentiment, it hurt the movement more than it helped.

King eventually was enjoined from entering the building or

interfering with its operations. He was told not to collect any more rent and to give an accounting of the moneys that had been collected. The court also appointed a receiver for the building.

The Chicago campaign continued to move slowly and at times to flounder during those first few months while the King and Daley forces sparred with each other. During this period King was actually only a part-time resident in Chicago. In addition to the demands that impacted the life of the 1964 national civil rights leader and the international commitments of a Nobel Peace Prize winner, King also insisted on spending three days a week in Atlanta, where he maintained his identity as the co-pastor of Ebenezer Baptist Church.

It was also becoming increasingly obvious that although the SCLC staff members had attempted to lay the groundwork for the Chicago campaign before King's arrival, they had not done a sufficiently thorough job with their homework. Lack of sufficient planning, apathy of the people, unfamiliarity with northern terrain, lack of unity among King's advisers, and the absence of a living, breathing hate symbol—the role that Bull Connor in Birmingham, Jim Clark in Selma, and to a lesser degree Laurie Pritchett in Albany had played in the Southern campaigns—were all factors which affected the slow development of the Chicago campaign.

At various times during the campaign, Mayor Daley would upstage King by initiating proposals of his own. For example, shortly after King arrived in Chicago and shortly before his assumption of the trusteeship of the old tenement building, the city announced its plan for a new drive against slumlords. On May 26, the same day that the Chicago papers carried an announcement by King about a proposed demonstration to protest the shooting of a black candidate for alderman, the procurement of a sizable HUD (Housing and Urban Development) loan to the city to renovate five hundred substandard apartment units was also made. Daley's office announced that slums would be ended within the decade. At another point in the campaign, when King was planning a mass rally at Soldier Field in Chicago and upbraiding city officials for their lack of action, Daley proposed and mobilized his administration to secure the passage of a $195 million bond issue for capital improvements. *The New York Times* noted that Daley had always used the strategy of implementing the program of his opponent with alarming success. Toward the beginning of the campaign the *Times* stated: "If Daley makes a mistake, it will not be for lack of interest in the slums. He has always beaten his enemies by taking their programs and running with them. Before he's through, his crusade will make King's look minor league."[3]

The summer taught King and his wife a lesson on the impact of the ghetto upon the lives of young children. During the summer the King children, who had stayed in Atlanta in order to avoid any interruption of their school year, came to Chicago to stay with their parents in the Lawndale ghetto. However, after only a few days the Kings noticed a change in their children's behavior. As their tempers flared and one of their sons became almost unmanageable, the Kings realized that crowded living conditions within the flat were about to produce an emotional explosion within their own family. King wrote:

> It was just too hot, too crowded, too devoid of creative forms of recreation. There was just not space enough in the neighborhood to run off the energy of childhood without running into busy, traffic-laden streets. And I understood anew the conditions which make of the ghetto an emotional pressure cooker.[4]

The King children were soon sent back to the fresh air of middle-class Atlanta.

On Sunday, July 26, King launched another phase of the Chicago movement and directly assaulted the city's housing conditions by holding a huge rally at Soldier Field. King had expected around 100,000 people to attend. SCLC estimated the actual crowd to be around 45,000 persons. The police estimated the attendance to be only 23,000. King had announced that marches would take place through the white suburbs of Chicago.

Two days after King's Soldier Field Rally a riot erupted on Chicago's west side when the police attempted to turn off a fire hydrant that some children had activated. A fight ensued, and the volatile black ghetto exploded once again. As King sought to use his presence and influence to restore order, he was faced with another difference between Chicago and Birmingham. Coretta King wrote: "Chicago is such a big city, and we were so few, that our effectiveness was diminished. Once violence starts, it is contagious. The problem was that we had to deal, not with one neighborhood, but with pockets of people scattered over an enormous area."[5]

When the riots subsided, King began to escalate the movement by launching a series of marches through white neighborhoods. On Friday, August 5, Al Raby, a local community leader, and gospel singer Mahalia Jackson led seven hundred demonstrators across Ashland Avenue, where real estate groups had contained blacks for years, to Marquette Park, where King had planned to picket a white real estate agent. When the demonstrators arrived, they were greeted by American Nazi Party leader George Lincoln Rockwell and a group of jeering whites. When King arrived on the scene, the jeers turned to violence. Rocks, bricks, bottles, and other missiles were thrown through the air; King himself was hit by a brick. The marchers fled back across Ashland Avenue as the police fought back the attacking whites. After eight months of searching for the tender nerve of the city, King had learned that it was real estate. The white community with its little houses on its little plots of ground and its little lawns was adamant about not yielding any of its "turf" to black encroachment. The residential areas of the black and white communities were as tightly insulated and as rigidly segregated in the North as they were in the South. As terrifying as they were, the riots had not frightened the whites, since the blacks had burned their own buildings and looted the shops in their own neighborhood. The whites were frightened by the prospect of black neighbors. It would be the tender real estate nerve that King would rub raw by his marches into lily-white communities. The hate which was induced had a different accent to be sure, but it was as vehement as in the South.

A march through the white Gage Park section produced some violence. Another march into the Belmont-Cragin area resulted in still more violence. A surprise march into the downtown Loop and simultaneous marches into the Gage, Bogan, and Jefferson Park communities brought even more bitter and violent reactions from whites. Mayor Daley sent an emissary to King's apartment with the proposal that if the demonstrations were halted, then the city would hire some three hundred persons, who were to come from the ranks of the tenants, as housing guards. The city also promised to construct a few hundred new apartment units and hire one black journeyman glazier for the housing authority.

King, however, rejected the mayor's proposal.

King did agree to a meeting involving other high-ranking clergymen, business leaders, real estate boards, union leaders, and politicians. At this meeting the SCLC called for the enforcement of the city's open housing laws, the suspension of the licenses of real estate brokers who were guilty of discriminatory sales, and the withdrawal of a suit sponsored by the Chicago Real Estate Board before the Illinois Supreme Court contesting the legality of the state's open housing. Although the meeting lasted a full eight hours, no agreement that was acceptable to both sides was reached. When another meeting held two days later failed to reach any definitive agreement, Mayor Daley announced that the city was seeking legal redress against the demonstrators. An injunction was issued which limited the demonstrations to one per day, restricted the number of participants to five hundred, and required a written twenty-four-hour advance notice to be submitted to the police superintendent. In addition, night marches and demonstrations during the peak traffic rush hours were proscribed. King labelled the city's efforts "unjust, illegal, and unconstitutional," but instead of violating the injunction, he chose to fight it in the courts. It should be noted that in this contest against Mayor Daley, King received no support from the White House, for by this time he had begun to speak out against the Vietnam war, thus alienating the Johnson administration.

Faced with the increasing intransigence of the Daley political machine and knowing that no federal help was forthcoming, the movement leaders decided to employ what was considered to be their potentially most effective and certainly most risky and dangerous plan. King announced that he would lead a march into the community of Cicero, which was not in Chicago but in Cook County, and therefore not subject to the injunction.

Cicero, the home away from home for the infamous gangster Al Capone and other mobsters, was a completely white community composed of lower middle-class homeowners of Slavic descent. The last time a black family had attempted to move into Cicero had been fifteen years earlier, at which time a race riot erupted. Sheriff Richard Ogilvie referred to the march as "suicidal," and Governor Otto Kerner placed the National Guard and the state police on ready alert.

Increasing political pressures, escalating tensions, and polarization on both sides prompted city officials to reopen negotiations. Two days before the march, an announcement was made that an agreement had been reached in which the real estate board agreed to withdraw all opposition to the philosophy of open housing legislation at the state level, provided it was applicable to owners as well as brokers. However, although the real estate board agreed to withdraw its opposition to the philosophy of open housing legislation, it did not withdraw its appeal before the Cook County circuit court against the city's fair housing ordinances. The city housing authority pledged to begin placing families in the best possible neighborhoods without regard to the racial composition of the neighborhood. Punitive action, such as revocation or suspension of brokerage licenses, was to be taken against those brokers who failed to comply with fair housing policies. The bankers also pledged to adopt a nondiscriminatory policy of lending money. Catholic, Protestant, and Jewish groups pledged their support in securing equal access to housing for all people. King referred to the agreement as the strongest step ever taken in the nation to secure equal access to housing and agreed to "defer" the march in Cicero. Militants from CORE and SNCC referred to the agreement as a "sellout."

The Chicago campaign, like the Albany movement, taught King some painful lessons about his nonviolent ethic. First, it exposed its geographic limitations. The size, geographical distribution, and political complexities of the Northern urban areas presented new problems. King recognized these difficulties when he wrote:

Nonviolence must be adapted to urban conditions and urban moods. The effectiveness of street marches in cities is limited because the normal turbulence of city life absorbs them as mere transitory drama quite common in the ordinary movement of the masses. In the South, a march was a social earthquake; in the North, it is a faint, brief exclamation of protest.[6]

Second, the Chicago campaign exposed the programmatic limitations of King's nonviolent ethic. We have noted that King was aware that the issues of the second phase of the movement were more complex than those involving the abrogation of constitutional rights, which were addressed in the first decade of the struggle. Yet King attacked the complex problems related to racism and economic justice with the same battle plan that was used in the Southern civil rights campaigns. When the agenda was changed and new issues and a new set of problems were proposed and when the goals of the struggle were redefined and a new constituency formed, one needed seriously to consider new solutions and new strategies.

The problem of the Chicago campaign, then, was not that it did not follow the pattern of nonviolent protest that began in Montgomery and was further refined in Birmingham and Selma. The problem of the Chicago campaign was that, given the new complexities of both the urban context and the issues related to economic justice, it followed the script too closely. In his book *Where Do We Go from Here: Chaos or Community?* which was written after the Chicago campaign, King attempted to make some specific programmatic suggestions regarding education, housing, and employment. Thus, the Chicago experience helped King to rethink and redefine his nonviolent ethic.

The Vietnam War

The year 1965 was the year that Watts exploded almost upon the heel of the passage of the Voting Rights Act; it was also the year the Nobel Peace Prize winner of 1964, Martin Luther King, Jr., began publicly to criticize the conduct of the Vietnam war under the Johnson administration. It was during this period that he made the statement:

> I'm not going to sit by and see war escalated without saying anything about it. . . . It is worthless to talk about integrating if there is no world to integrate in. . . . The war in Vietnam must be stopped. There must be a negotiated settlement even with the Viet Cong. . . . The long night of war must be stopped.[7]

When King first started speaking out against the Vietnam war, it has been said that President Johnson stormed around his office saying: "What is that preacher doing to me? We gave him the Civil Rights Act of 1964, we gave him the Voting Rights Act of 1965, we gave him the War on Poverty. What more does he want?"[8]

Although King surprised President Johnson and a number of others with his stance on Vietnam, a careful reading of some of his writings will show that his strong opinions about the subject of war were not new. In 1958 King said that nuclear tests should cease. Because of the tremendous destructive potential of war both to living and future generations, he felt that the goal of all nations must be the total abandonment of the concept of war and a firm commitment to disarmament. Either war must be eliminated or humankind will be eliminated.[9] In *Stride Toward Freedom*, he wrote that the black American with his nonviolent methodology could possibly provide the world with a desperately needed alternative to war. In *Why We Can't Wait*, King decried the principle of war and stressed nonviolence as a necessary corrective for a world which has within its grasp the possibilities of its own destruction.[10] In *Strength to Love*, King stated that at one time he looked upon war as a negative good which could be used to check the spread of evil. War, he felt, just might be preferable to an abdication to totalitarianism. However, the potential destructive power of today's weapons has ruled out the possibility of war being even a negative good. He felt that he could not remain silent as long as humankind faced the threat of nuclear annihilation and that to be true to its mission, the church must call for an end to the arms race.[11]

When King received the Nobel Peace Prize, he stated that the demands for his participation in both national and international affairs had grown, and even though he would continue to devote most of his energies to the South and its problems, he would also do more work outside of the South, becoming more involved in the racial problems of the urban North. He further stated that he would intensify his attention to the three great problems facing humankind: racism, poverty, and war. King felt that black America was a small part of a worldwide revolt against racial injustice. As a Nobel Peace Prize winner, he felt a commitment to spread the nonviolent philosophy to all exploited people of the world who were struggling to throw off the yoke of racial oppression.

Red China's acquisition of the atomic bomb was an indicator to King that the nations of the world were not reducing, but increasing, their stockpiles of weapons for mass destruction. Humankind's propensity to engage in war was still a fact. However, the lesson to be derived from the most recent conflagration (i.e., Vietnam) was that the concept of war was obsolete. An alternative to war must be found because humankind has a right to survive, and any attempt to engage in war today would leave only "the smoldering ashes of an inferno."[12]

King also found strong support for his involvement with the peace effort from his wife. Coretta King had been very active in the Women's Strike for Peace and the Women's International League for Peace and Freedom. During the period in which he attempted to separate the peace and civil rights movements, his wife made a number of speeches on Vietnam for him.

Although King had held strong views on war for a number of years and although he was heartened by being awarded the Nobel Peace Prize and by his wife's encouragement to articulate his views, the decision to speak out against the Vietnam war was, nevertheless, a difficult one to make. According to Andrew Young, King went through a long period of prayer and fasting before he decided to participate actively in the peace movement. There were several considerations that made King hesitant. First, he was concerned about the effect of further dissipating his already limited time and overtaxed energies from the civil rights movement. Second, he was not as familiar with the peace movement, nor as sure of himself within it, as he was in the freedom movement. He had helped to shape the freedom movement. At one time the freedom movement had been identified with his name. Although he had lost credibility among some whites and was regarded as passé by a number of blacks, he was still respected for his initial contribution to the movement.

The same thing could not be said about King's involvement with the peace movement. He did not light its fire, nor did he shape it or help determine its philosophy or goals, nor was he a determinative influence in the structure or organization of the movement. Much of the terrain was already selected before he associated himself with it. The peace movement had its own vocabulary, its own goals, and its own constituency. King was also sensitive to persons within the peace movement who wanted to exploit his name to enhance the credibility of the peace effort.

In addition, King was concerned about the possible negative effect that his participation in the peace movement would have upon the civil rights struggle, with particular regard to the Johnson administration. King's hesitation was based upon his assessment of the power inherent in the office of the presidency rather than on a personal commitment or gratitude to President Johnson. King felt that the office of the president held executive powers and resources which could be directed toward ending institutional racism in America. He felt that no president had ever done much for the black American and that both President John F. Kennedy and President Lyndon B. Johnson had been given a great deal of unmerited credit. The administrations of both Kennedy and Johnson happened to coincide with the period of social ferment by blacks. Neither Kennedy nor Johnson voluntarily submitted civil rights legislation. At one time they both stated that such legislation was impossible. Although Johnson, in response to the spirit of the period, had used his skills as a legislator to push bills through Congress, in King's view he had not been very diligent in the implementation of the legislation that had been enacted during his administration. Thus, King had no personal commitment to President Johnson. However, he was politically astute enough to know that the freedom movement needed the support of the president of the United States. Therefore, he thought long and deeply about the consequences that would accrue to the movement because of his stand on Vietnam.

King, however, reached a point in his inner struggle where, political considerations notwithstanding, he felt that silence on a matter about which he felt so strongly and had such grave misgivings was a compromise of his convictions. King's reasons for opposing the war were consistent with the various components of his nonviolent ethics. They were consistent with the prophetic tradition of the black religious experience. His reasons were consistent with Walter Rauschenbusch's social gospel theology that underscored the Christian's contention with "principalities and powers." They were consistent with Brightman's personalistic philosophy that stressed the sanctity of personality and the inviolability of personhood for any reason under any circumstances. They were consistent with King's personal commitment to nonviolence as a philosophy and as a way of life. His reasons were consistent with his commitment to nonviolence as an appropriate strategy in international relationships, as well as social and political relationships on the national level. They were consistent with his concern about economic injustice and racism, both of which were being perpetuated by the Vietnam war.

Consequently, on April 4, 1967, at Riverside Church in New York City, King delivered his most detailed and comprehensive speech in which he stated his reasons for opposing the Vietnam war. In addition to identifying the Nobel Peace Prize as a personal commission to work for the "brotherhood of man," King gave other reasons for opposing the Vietnam war. First, he asserted that there was a connection between the war in Vietnam and the War on Poverty in America. The Vietnam war was the enemy of the poor in that it drained the War on Poverty of the national resources—human skills, funds, and administrative commitment—needed to rehabilitate the poor. The devastating impact of the war upon economic justice was of paramount importance to King.

Second, the war was not only destroying the hopes of the poor by draining their communities of vital programmatic monies, it was also sending their sons to Vietnam to fight and die in numbers that were excessively out of proportion with the rest of the population. Related to the war's economic injustice was its racism. Although King was concerned about the way that the war discriminated against the poor generally, he was particularly sensitive to its effects upon the black poor. He noted that among the proportionately higher numbers of the poor who were doing the first-line fighting was still a greater number of blacks. Although he felt that the war discriminated against certain socioeconomic classes, he did not discount racism as a possible factor in its inequities. The United States foreign policy, in King's opinion, was the result of racist decision making. The culture of the white West was so thoroughly racist that it warped the perspectives of those who were shaped by it, whether they like it or not, toward those of darker hue.

Third, King also stressed inconsistencies and contradictions inherent in the involvement of blacks in the Vietnam war. He stated that young blacks who had been crippled by this society were sent 8,000 miles away to protect the very liberties in Southeast Asia that had been withheld from them in Southwest Georgia and East Harlem, and that blacks and whites could kill and die together for a nation that had been unwilling to seat them together in the same school.

Fourth, King also felt that it was ideologically contradictory and theoretically inconsistent to advocate nonviolence domestically while condoning violence abroad. King's experience in working with Chicago youth helped him reach the conclusion that integrity and intellectual honesty required that he be consistent in his views on nonviolence. When King had sought to persuade Chicago ghetto youth to seek social change through nonviolence, they had asked him about Vietnam and the nation's attempt to solve its problems through violence. King also felt that he was being true to the spirit and purposes of SCLC. The motto of SCLC was "to save the soul of America." Since the Vietnam war was destroying the soul of America, King saw no inconsistency between his role as civil rights leader and that of spokesman for the peace movement.

More personally significant for King was his feeling that he was being true to his commitments to his ministry—whose message of reconciliation and peace went beyond national allegiances—and to his Lord, Jesus Christ, who loved his enemies so much that he prayed for their forgiveness. This Lord summoned all people to the worship of the heavenly Creator who is especially concerned for the suffering, helpless, and outcast. Thus, King felt a moral commitment to speak for the weak, the voiceless, the victimized, and those who may be regarded by the nation as enemies but with whom is shared the brotherhood and sisterhood of humanity and the fatherhood and motherhood of God.

After the personal, theological, ethical, and philosophical reasons for his opposition to the war, King next criticized the nature of the involvement that the United States historically had in the affairs of Vietnam. He defined that involvement as being essentially oppressive, colonialistic, and antirevolutionary. Considering the damage that the United States had done to the people, the land, and the culture of Vietnam, the United States, rather than the Vietnamese compatriots, was regarded as the enemy. When the United States compared its claim to be friend and supporter of the people with its track record in Vietnam, the United States had to emerge as a strange liberator. He said:

> We have destroyed their two most cherished institutions: the family and the village. We have destroyed their land and their crops. We cooperated in the crushing of the nation's only noncommunist rev-

olutionary political force—the unified Buddhist Church. We have supported the enemies of the peasants of Saigon. We have corrupted their women and children and killed their men. What liberators![13]

King felt that the war was equally as damaging and dehumanizing to the American troops. He called for a cessation of America's escalation of the war and placed the onus for negotiation on the United States.

King further stated that Vietnam was symptomatic of a deeper malady of the American spirit which had put the United States on the wrong side of a world revolution against colonialism and oppression. Increasingly, the United States by its policies in Guatemala, Peru, Mozambique, South Africa, Columbia, Venezuela, Thailand, and Cambodia had shown itself to be a counterrevolutionary force that refused to give up the privileges and pleasures that come from the immense profits of overseas investments. In order for the United States to get on the right side of the world revolution, the nation must undergo "a radical revolution of values" which would change it from a "thing-oriented" to a "person-oriented" society.

A revolution of values would also mean that Americans would become ecumenical rather than sectarian, cosmopolitan rather than provincial. Americans must develop an overriding loyalty to humankind which lifts neighborly concern beyond one's class, tribe, race, or nation. The key to this overriding loyalty would be an all-embracing and unconditional love for all people. King felt that the time for this kind of revolution was at hand, since delay could only spell doom for humankind. He wrote:

> In this unfolding conundrum of life and history there is such a thing as being too late. . . . The "tide in the affairs of men" does not remain at the flood; it ebbs. . . . Over the bleached bones and jumbled residue of numerous civilizations are written the pathetic words: "Too late." There is an invisible book of life that faithfully records our vigilance or our neglect. "The moving finger writes, and having written moves on. . . ." We still have a choice today; nonviolent coexistence or violent co-annihilation.[14]

The reaction to King's speech in Riverside Church was, as could be expected, mixed. King's earlier statements about the war had already made him *persona non grata* to the Johnson administration. The Riverside Church speech, therefore, only exacerbated an already damaged relationship. Some of the harshest criticism, however, came from leading blacks who had been King's colleagues and allies in the freedom struggle. The NAACP Board voted unanimously against any efforts to blend the civil rights and the peace movements. Former Nobel Peace Prize winner Dr. Ralph Bunche stated that King "should positively and publicly give up one role or the other."[15] Carl Rowan, a black professional journalist and syndicated columnist, wrote a stinging criticism of King's antiwar position.

King and Whitney Young, the executive director of the Urban League, had already publicly disagreed on the Vietnam issue. In March 1967 King and Young attended a fund-raising dinner in Great Neck, New York. The Vietnam issue came up, and King stated his criticism of the war. Young stated that the Urban League was interested in fighting the other war in the ghetto and that it was his personal opinion that communism had to be checked today just as Hitler had to be stopped during World War II. Toward the close of the evening Young and King became involved in a brief but very intense argument. Young told King that his position was tactically and politically unwise, to which the SCLC leader replied, "Whitney, what you're saying may get you a foundation grant, but it won't get you into the kingdom of truth." Young felt that he, rather than King, had the viable programs for urban communities. He questioned the sincerity of King's interest in the ghettos. Young looked at King and said, "You're eating well." King insisted that one of the reasons that he opposed the war was because of the damage that it was doing to the ghetto. The argument became so heated that King's lawyer broke it up.[16]

Not only was the black civil rights leadership unresponsive to King's position on Vietnam, but the black community itself was, for the most part, cool in its response to King's involvement with the peace movement. Louis Lomax has rightly observed that the Vietnam protests, "while a source of passionate concern to Martin Luther King, seemed to leave the overwhelming majority of Negroes cold (and, in all frankness, the same statement would have to be made for the parades to support our men in Vietnam)."[17] When he was in Selma and Birmingham, King's fiery oratory inspired blacks in large numbers to march, make contributions, and go to jail. When it came to the Vietnam war and the peace movement, even with King's leadership, charisma, and rhetorical gifts, black participation remained relatively minor in scope.

Vietnam may not have been a major issue among blacks because blacks on a daily basis had to fight other battles that were more immediate and more pressing. Unemployment or underemployment; racism, both institutional and personal; black-on-black crime; the lack of equitable delivery of municipal services; police corruption, mediocrity, and brutality; traffic in drugs; inadequate medical care; substandard housing and inferior schools—these were the concerns which affected the lives of black people on a daily basis more than Vietnam. Although black families were touched in a personal way when one of their members was drafted or maimed or killed in the war, the struggle to survive daily, weekly, and monthly, year in and year out was so intense that Vietnam appeared to be a remote issue. Whitney Young correctly observed, "The Negro is more concerned about the rat at night and the job in the morning than he is about the war in Vietnam."[18]

If Vietnam alienated King from some of his traditional allies and left the bulk of the rank and file of black Americans unmoved, it also provided, from a practical standpoint, an opportunity for him to recoup the prestige and credibility lost through the rise of the younger black militants and the outcome of the Chicago campaign. It also afforded him a way to regain his constituency among liberal, antiwar whites who had become estranged from the movement with the advent of black power. Vietnam not only held the potential of reuniting King and liberal, antiwar whites but also ironically linked King and black radicals like Stokely Carmichael who had already come out against the war.

The practical advantages of King's adopting an antiwar stance and the possibility of other motivating factors at work in King's psyche besides prophetic compulsion or righteous indignation do not take away from the integrity of King's commitment to peace. Once when King had responded to one of his former allies who had criticized his stand on Vietnam, he turned to his wife and said: "I know I'm right. I know this is an unjust and evil war. I have made my decision to oppose it, and whatever people say, I am going to stick to my convictions."[19]

There were those who questioned King's opposition to the

Vietnam war because they really believed that peace and civil rights were separate movements and ought not be combined. There were others, however, who took umbrage at the audacity of a black who "got out of his place" and either raised questions or spoke definitively on matters of foreign policy. King, who was a strategist, and at times a pragmatist, as well as a moralist, certainly must have known that the price was too high and the risks too great for a face-saving, credibility-restoring ego trip. When one is black, one does not oppose the president of the United States and the sentiment of white middle America, which finances black civil rights organizations, and expect to win. To do so is truly to risk all. Black author John Williams, in his reflections on the implications of King's stand on Vietnam, has written:

> It seems to me that King broke with whatever compromise he might have made when he jumped into the Vietnam War protest, determined to sock it to those who would have restrained him. And when he made his decision, he must have known that his life, although he had been threatened time and time again, was now measured.[20]

Historically, black men who have dealt in foreign policy for whatever reasons, whether at home or abroad, have encountered hostility. "One thinks back to men like William Monroe Trotter; W. E. B. DuBois; to Marcus Garvey, although he wasn't in the same class; to Malcolm X, who was learning as he went; their fates were distressingly similar, perhaps suspiciously similar. Exile, accidental death, assassination. . . ."[21] Although the entire blame ought not be placed on the Vietnam war, it is worth noting that on April 4, 1968, exactly one year after his "Vietnam and the Struggle for Human Rights" speech, Martin Luther King, Jr., was dead.

Summary

After Selma, then, the issues of economic justice and international peace coalesced to become the foci of King's nonviolent ethic. King's move to Chicago and his stand on the Vietnam war were not simply two more practical applications of his nonviolent ethic but represented the broadening of its theoretical framework as well. Although these two issues came into focus after Selma, they were part of King's ethical perspective long were not simply two more practical applications of his nonviolent ethic but represented the broadening of its theoretical framework as well. Although these two issues came into focus after Selma, they were part of King's ethical perspective long before Selma. King was not a doctrinaire capitalist and had at times debated with his father about the basics of capitalism as he questioned what he perceived to be the injustices inherent in the system.

At various times during his career King had spoken to the issue of peace. There were periods in his life when King devoted more of his time and attention to economic justice than to peace and vice versa. Both of these concerns, however, simultaneously shared the center of King's theological perspective and ethical consciousness.

At the time King was assassinated, he was one of the leading critics of the Vietnam war and one of the most venerated spokespersons for the international peace movement. When he was assassinated, he was also fighting for the rights of striking garbage workers in Memphis, Tennessee, and was in the midst of testing the idea of the Poor Peoples' March to Washington, D.C., to dramatize the plight of the nation's poor. His life, the witness of his ethic, and his death embodied the twin themes, "no peace without justice" and "no justice without peace."

5

The Six Principles
of the Nonviolent Ethic
# of Martin Luther King, Jr.

Martin Luther King's nonviolent ethic, as it evolved out of the Montgomery struggle and was developed by application and refined by experience, consisted basically of six major principles. King delineated these principles in his book *Stride Toward Freedom*.[1] Although this book was written in the early days of King's engagement with nonviolence as a method to effect social change, and although experience and an expanded ethical perspective continued to redefine King's priorities and reshape his thinking, these six principles remained the central, integrating, constituent elements of his nonviolent ethic.

Nonviolence, the Weapon of the Strong

The first principle listed by King is that nonviolence is the way of the strong, not a method for the cowardly. Persons who use the nonviolent method of protest either because they are afraid or because they lack the instruments of violence are not truly nonviolent.

This principle was undoubtedly appropriated from Gandhi, who also stated that nonviolence was the method of the strong.

Both King and Gandhi were referring to inner, spiritual strength rather than outward, physical force. When one's inclination is to respond to violence with violence, a strong sense of purpose and commitment to the cause for which one is suffering, a great deal of discipline and self-restraint, and a strong self-image are essential for a nonviolent response to acts of aggression without an accompanying feeling of defeat and powerlessness. Nonviolence thus becomes a method of the strong. When one reflects upon the courage of an unarmed resister who faces an armed opponent, nonviolence becomes a method for the brave, rather than the cowardly.

One should never forget that Gandhi's situation was different from King's just as the Indian experience in India was different from the black experience in America. The numerical advantage of the Indians in their campaign against British domination made Gandhi's assertion about nonviolence and strength plausible for several reasons. First, numerical advantage in a struggle can fortify inner strength. Second, numerical advantage also means that one has a realistic option of alternative methods and strategies of resistance. Third, the Indians were being colonized in their native land by a foreign oppressor. In India, Gandhi could always tell the oppressor to "go home!" The Indians were the majority group and the oppressing British were the minority. Although they had no weaponry, their status as the native residents and their position of numerical advantage could have provided some kind of psychological leverage had Gandhi opted for violence.

In the United States the black American was "domestically" colonized. Harold Cruse stated that instead of the United States establishing a colonial empire in Africa, it brought the system home and established it in the antebellum South. From the viewpoint of the architects of the system, black Americans were not the "we" but the "they." The factor which differentiated the black American's status from the traditional colonial being was that the black American resided in the "home" country in close proximity to the dominant oppressing group.[2] American blacks as a minority group oppressed by hostile majority home rule did not operate from a position of numerical advantage. The Indians outnumbered the British one thousand to one. There were enough Indian bodies literally to form a wall against the imperialistic British and stop them from functioning if the Indians had so chosen. Black Americans, on the other hand, were outnumbered nine to one.[3] They could not tell the oppressor to "go home" since they were the ones who were looked upon as outsiders, or at least as troublesome appendages, by the majority group. Whenever American blacks protested or marched, although they were at home, they did so in an atmosphere of hostility, as aliens in an alien land, with whites assuming the role of domestic rulers.

King's statement that only those who have a choice of other strategies and means of resistance are truly nonviolent has caused some to question the character of the nonviolence of those black Americans who participated in the civil rights campaign under the banner of SCLC. Since black Americans did not have a realistic violent option, one could question whether there ever was a true nonviolent movement among them.

Novelist John Killens has declared that the "non-violent Negro" is a myth and that "the only reason black men have not long ago resorted to violence is that white men have the more powerful weapon and the greater numbers."[4]

Although King might have argued that black Americans had the option of a violent methodology, his basic position was that violence was such a self-defeating, no-win strategy that he wrote it off as being both immoral and impractical.

The lack of a violent option notwithstanding, King could argue with much effectiveness that, particularly for black Americans, nonviolence was still a credible, potent, and effective method for social and political change even for those lacking realistic alternatives of protest and resistance. Social ethicist Reinhold Niebuhr, for example, emphasized the feasibility of a nonviolent methodology in situations of group powerlessness when he stated that "non-violence is a particularly strategic instrument for an oppressed group which is hopelessly in the minority and has no possibility of developing sufficient power to set against its oppressors."[5] It was precisely because blacks lacked the numerical strength and the options which that advantage made possible that nonviolence became the weapon of the strong.

When one considers all the disadvantages that were a part of the existential situation of black Americans, to protest at all required a great deal of courage, determination, and inner resolve.

Since nonviolence, in King's view, represented strength rather than weakness, it was not to be confused with "stagnant passivity" because nonviolence does resist. King felt that the term "passive resistance" was a misnomer because it implied a "do-nothing method" that encouraged acquiescence to evil and had led persons like Reinhold Niebuhr to misinterpret the pacifist position. Niebuhr, in King's opinion, had interpreted pacifism as a "sort of passive nonresistance to evil expressing naive trust in the power of love."[6] King felt that this was a serious distortion of pacifism. The nonviolent resister was passive in the sense that he or she was not physically aggressive or violent toward the opponent. At the same time, the emotions and the mind were activated as resisters sought to convince the opponent that he or she was wrong. The nonviolent resister, consequently, was spiritually active. King's pacifism, then, was not a passive nonresistance to evil but an active, nonviolent resistance to evil. He insisted that Gandhi had resisted evil with as much passion and conviction as the person who adhered to a violent methodology; Gandhi simply resisted with love instead of with hate. In describing his position, King wrote:

> True pacifism is not unrealistic submission to evil power, as Niebuhr contends. It is rather a courageous confrontation of evil by the power of love, in the faith that it is better to be the recipient of violence than the inflicter of it, since the latter only multiplies the existence of violence and bitterness in the universe, while the former may develop a sense of shame in the opponent, and thereby bring about a transformation and change of heart.[7]

Reconciliation, the Goal of Nonviolence

The second major principle of King's nonviolent philosophy is that the goal of nonviolent resistance is always redemption and reconciliation. The goal of nonviolence is not the humiliation or defeat of the opponent but the winning of the enemy's friendship and understanding.

Although the nonviolent resister might protest through boycotts and noncooperation, these are not ends but means to stir the conscience of the opponent or awaken in the opponent a sense of moral shame. Bitterness, hatred, and brokenness are the aftermath of violence. Wholeness, healing, and the creation of the beloved community are the fruits of nonviolence. If the Montgomery bus boycott and the Birmingham and Selma campaigns are to be credited as victories for King's nonviolent ethic, then one must understand that reconciliation, redemption, and the creation of the beloved community were long-range ideals rather than immediately attainable goals. After the Supreme Court issued the bus desegregation order, a number of churches and private homes were bombed in Montgomery's black community. Birmingham's Sixteenth Street Baptist Church was bombed after the nonviolent campaign there. A white woman from Detroit who was working within the Selma voter registration drive was shot to death on the very night that the mammoth march to Montgomery ended. Although white moderates spoke out against the terrorist excesses of white extremists, their pleas were for the restoration of order rather than for justice due to blacks.

Although his rhetoric may have led his hearers or readers to believe that he considered reconciliation to be immediate rather than distant in its realization—and at the beginning he probably thought that, if not imminent, it was not as distant as it turned out to be—King was aware that the beloved community would not be an instantaneous creation. He wrote:

> This method of nonviolence will not work miracles overnight. Men are not easily moved from their mental ruts, their prejudiced and irrational feelings. When the underprivileged demand freedom, the privileged first react with bitterness and resistance. Even when the demands are couched in nonviolent terms, the initial response is the same. . . . In the South too, the initial white reaction to Negro resistance has been bitter. I do not predict that a similar happy ending will come to Montgomery in a few months, because integration is more complicated than independence.[8]

Although one could debate which was more complicated—integration or independence—King's point here was that although nonviolence could facilitate the process, the reconciliation of broken communities was a complex, difficult, and time-consuming task, especially when there was resistance to change.

Ideally reconciliation like *agape* (love), which will be discussed later, is a process that is free of coercive elements. The apostle Paul in his declaration of the new being in Christ also expressed the essence of the theology of the crucifixion when he wrote,

"All this is from God, who through Christ reconciled us to himself . . . not counting their trespasses against them, and entrusting to us the message of reconciliation" (2 Corinthians 5:18-19, RSV). At Calvary God set the example of how costly reconciliation and redemption can be. While the price of God's only Son is a dear one to pay for the restoration of broken linkages, it is not too great for divine *agape*. Yet with all the pain involved in the reconciliation of creation with Creator, human beings are free to accept or reject God's "unspeakable gift." Human beings are still called or invited rather than conscripted into the kingdom. The kerygma (the preaching of the gospel), with all of its missionary intent, still ends with an invitation, rather than a demand, that essentially says, "Whosoever will, let him or her come."

Those who work nonviolently and otherwise on behalf of reconciliation and redemption often find themselves in situations of conflict occasioned by those who resist change. For a number of individuals the pain that change brings and the threat to security that comes with newness are prices too dear to pay. Therefore, the elements of pressure and coercion enter the process. Social ethicist Roger Shinn has written:

> It is doubtful that a power elite ever gives in without some kind of pressure. I do not mean that people in power are always brutul cynics. They may want to do right. But they see issues from their perspective. Naturally they want to preserve old values, move cautiously, avoid any damage in the changeover. They are not highly sensitive to the pain of those who suffer injustice and cannot enjoy the values of the dominant group. Loving parents are reluctant to give freedom to children without some pressure from below. Benevolent despots rarely grant rights to their subjects without pressure. And moral white people, who do not themselves suffer the harshness of discrimination, are unlikely to act boldly until they feel pressure from those who do suffer.[9]

Thus, while maintaining its commitment to reconciliation, nonviolent resistance involves coercion. The coercion may be nonviolent, but it coerces nevertheless. In the view of Reinhold Niebuhr, nonviolence was not as morally pure as many interpreted it to be because it often resulted in the same social effects as violence. He felt that "non-violent conflict and coercion may also result in the destruction of life or property and they usually do. The difference is that destruction is not the intended but the inevitable consequence of non-violent coercion."[10] He concluded:

> Non-co-operation, in other words, results in social consequences not totally dissimilar from those of violence. The differences are very important; but before considering them it is necessary to emphasize the similarities and to insist that non-violence does coerce and destroy.[11]

Political scientist Hanes Walton has observed that all violence is not physical and that a kind of psychological violence, committed by nonphysical as well as physical acts, does injury to the integrity and dignity of both individuals and groups. Since violence can assume many forms in addition to the physical, such as the economic, spiritual, psychological, and countless subtle variations of these, Walton questioned whether it was possible to "expunge every taint of violence from one's actions, however well-intentioned they be." His line of argument led him to raise the same question about nonviolence as did Niebuhr: "Does not nonviolence as well as violence coerce by the pressures it brings to bear upon persons not yet ready for a radical change of outlook?"[12] The insights of Niebuhr and Walton on the coercive aspects of nonviolence were validated in King's application of it.

King was of the opinion that given the intransigence that he often found in the opponents he faced, coercion was a necessary element in the application of his nonviolent ethic. Although he continued to believe in the fundamental decency of human nature, and although he continued to appeal to the consciences of those who opposed him, he soon recognized that ethical appeals and moral suasion alone would not bring about justice for America's oppressed minorities. This was a point that Niebuhr had made many years earlier when he wrote: "It is hopeless for the Negro to expect complete emancipation from the menial social and economic position into which the white man has forced him, merely by trusting in the moral sense of the white race."[13] King insisted that ethical appeals must still be made because morality and power must go together "implementing, fulfilling, and ennobling each other."

While recognizing the legitimacy of ethical appeals, he also believed that "those appeals must be undergirded by some form of constructive coercive power."[14] Without the application of persistent pressure the black American would end up "empty-handed."

King did not consider nonviolent coercion to be anti-reconciliatory. Although tensions increased in those communities when and where the nonviolent method was used, King felt that nonviolence was not responsible for the estrangement and hostility between local blacks and whites. Nonviolence had simply unearthed latent and long-standing feelings of hostility. King believed that latent tensions first had to be unearthed, recognized, and dealt with before true reconciliation could occur. He often used the term "creative tension" to describe the process of healing, wholeness, and reconciliation brought about through the tension created when oppressed people demanded justice. Nonviolent resistance, pressure, and coercion simply helped to create the atmosphere in which the problem could be identified and dramatized and in which the solution could be sought. King would have agreed with Roger Shinn's point: "The changes in social organization make possible new experiences, which change the attitudes of people. Institutions can change hearts."[15]

Although the black and white communities have remained separate and largely unequal, some changes have occurred. Blacks, for example, are not intimidated by the white mystique as once they were. Both blacks and whites have learned to live with and accept some of the changes that have occurred during their lifetimes. These changes have heightened the sensitivities of persons in both communities to the subject of race and the existence of racism and have increased the dialogue between blacks and whites on individual bases. These changes have made it possible for blacks and whites to meet and know each other in settings of social equality; the affirmative action programs, which should be viewed as by-products of the ferment of the 1960s, have made it possible for them to relate to each other as equals in professional contexts and in work situations. These changes have also made it easier for some persons to cross the social and cultural barriers that historically have separated black from white and white from black; and persons in both communities have been able to build relationships and friendships based upon relative equality, mutual respect, trust, and *agape*. Perhaps it will be these persons and these relationships that will form the nucleus of King's beloved community.

Opponent as the Symbol of a Greater Evil

Not only did King depersonalize the goal of nonviolence by defining it in terms of reconciliation rather than the defeat of the opponent, but he also depersonalized the target of the nonviolent resister's attack. The third principle of King's ethic is that the opponent is a symbol of a greater evil.

Thus, nonviolence for King was directed against the forces of evil rather than against the persons who committed the evil. The evildoers were victims of evil as much as were the individuals and communities that the evildoers oppressed. According to King, the basic tension in Montgomery was not between whites and blacks but between justice and injustice and between the forces of light and the forces of darkness. The victory was not merely a victory for Montgomery's fifty thousand blacks but a triumph for justice and the forces of light. King conceptualized a defeat of injustice rather than a defeat of the white persons who may have been unjust.

King's perception of the movement as being one that was essentially "against principalities" rather than against persons had profound implications for the future development of his nonviolent ethic, particularly when it came to his inclusion of the controversial subject of the war in Vietnam as a matter of ethical concern. Herbert Richardson has written:

> The struggle against ideological conflict anywhere in the world is the struggle for the unity of men living together in the world. Conversely, because the struggle against racism is really a struggle against ideological conflict, Martin Luther King recognized that he had to oppose this kind of conflict wherever it appears. He was, so to say, under this obligation in principle. Hence, King was the first of those who linked the civil rights struggle to opposition to the Vietnam War.[16]

For King, the struggle "against principalities" included an asymmetry between the manifestation of evil and the manner in which it was opposed. A symmetry between the response and the manifestation would only perpetuate the existence of evil. "Returning violence for violence multiplies violence," wrote King, "adding deeper darkness to a night already devoid of stars. Darkness cannot drive out hate: only love can do that."[17] If humanity is to be advanced a step further, then violence must be rejected. The beauty of nonviolence in King's view was that it broke the chain reaction to evil and, with an ennobling sense of spiritual power, nonviolence elevated truth, beauty, and goodness from the scaffold to the throne. Only nonviolence that has been infused with love and ennobled by a sense of justice could provide the new power needed to set afoot a new humanity. Thus, violence must be met with nonviolence.

The distinction between the evils of a situation and the individuals who participated in them was an important one to make since, in the view of ethicist Reinhold Niebuhr, individuals are not as immoral as the social contexts in which they are involved and which they symbolize. However, Niebuhr also contended that "it is impossible completely to disassociate an evil system from the personal moral responsibilities of the individuals who maintain it."[18] Although one might argue for personal responsibility for social guilt, Niebuhr felt that it was morally and politically wrong to do so. For him, any benefit of the doubt given to the opponent would certainly reduce animosities and preserve some semblance of objectivity in assessing the disputed issue. Niebuhr did not consider resentments to be without value in a social struggle. A black person, for example, who resented racial injustice would do more to end it than the individual who experienced injustice without any emotional reactions. Niebuhr simply contended that resentment becomes a purer vehicle of justice when as many egoistic elements as possible are purged from it. He wrote: "The egoistic element in it may be objectively justified, but, from the perspective of an opponent in a social dispute, it never seems justified and merely arouses his own egotism."[19]

Hanes Walton, also pointing out the difficulty of depersonalizing the struggle against oppression, raised questions such as the following:

> How much of a person can actually be separated from his actions? And who, if not that person, is to be held responsible for those actions? . . . How is the evil perpetrated by one person to be distinguished from that bred by social institutions and their conditioning effects?[20]

Both Niebuhr and Walton allude to the fact that although one may intellectually, theoretically, and theologically make the distinction between the opponent as the source of evil and the opponent as a symbol of an evil source, in the realm of reality it is almost impossible to do so. When one is being beaten by a Jim Clark or hosed down by a Bull Connor, it is hard to believe that either of them is just as much a victim of an evil system as the one who is the recipient of their brutality.

Although King sought to depersonalize his campaigns by concentrating on the issues rather than the personalities involved, his nonviolent method worked best, as has been seen, in those situations in which there was a person who was a living embodiment of the evil system against whom sentiment could be molded. This was the role of Bull Connor in Birmingham and Jim Clark in Selma, where King was most successful. This was the role into which Laurie Pritchett and Richard Daley refused to be manipulated in Albany and Chicago, respectively, where King was less successful.

Redemptive Suffering

The fourth principle of King's nonviolent philosophy has to do with redemptive suffering. Nonviolence as conceptualized and understood by both Gandhi and King is based upon certain assumptions about power. It assumes that there is social and economic power in noncooperation and moral power in voluntary suffering for others. King's concept of redemptive (voluntary or creative) suffering assumes:

> (1) that there is power in withdrawing support from an evil or exploiting structure; (2) that opponents are human beings . . . to be respected and not violated; and (3) that the acceptance of suffering, rather than inflicting it on others, is itself a form of power, demoralizing to those who use violence without experiencing it in return and troublesome to the consciences of those who do not have an obvious vested interest in the maintenance of the system under attack.[21]

In King's view, the nonviolent resister had to be able to accept suffering without retaliating and accept blows without striking back. He continually stressed the educational possibilities of suffering and the redemptive potential of unearned suffering. In paraphrasing Gandhi, King said:

> We will match your capacity to inflict suffering with our capacity to endure suffering. We will meet your physical force with soul force. We will not hate you, but we cannot in all good conscience obey your unjust laws. Do to us what you will and we will still love you. Bomb

our homes and threaten our children; send your hooded perpetrators of violence into our communities and drag us out on some wayside road, beating us and leaving us half dead, and we will still love you. But we will soon wear you down by our capacity to suffer. And in winning our freedom we will appeal to your heart and conscience that we will win you in the process.[22]

King sought to answer those who believed that an oppressor who caused the innocent to suffer ought to be stopped by any means necessary and that failure to do so made one an accomplice to injury. He argued that a symmetrical response to a violent act led to legitimating everything from maiming a would-be rapist to an apology for the Vietnam war, thereby giving violence the hue of altruism by claiming it prevents suffering.

Its method is to inflict more suffering so that one must surrender unconditionally. King rejected this type of reasoning and insisted that suffering can be stopped only when it is endured rather than increased. In this way neither the personality of the oppressor nor that of the oppressed is violated. King insisted that this principle was applicable to the community, the nation, and the sphere of international relations, as well. King did not simply emphasize unmerited suffering. which blacks had already been experiencing for over 400 years, but emphasized creative suffering too. He urged people to accept the suffering that was intended for their degradation and wear it as a badge of honor. When one had learned to use the suffering that was designed for destruction as a means for liberation, then one would have learned how to suffer creatively.[23] Reinhold Niebuhr felt that although nonviolence involved coercion, its willingness to endure more pain than it inflicted made it a better method of producing moral goodwill than did violence. He wrote: "If non-violent resistance causes pain and suffering to the opposition, it mitigates the resentment, which such suffering usually creates, by enduring more pain than it inflicts."[24]

A number of persons had particular difficulty in accepting King's concept of creative suffering. John Oliver Killens, for example, stated that "there is no dignity for me in allowing another man to spit on me with impunity. There is no dignity for him or me. There is only sickness, and it will beget an even greater sickness. It degrades me and brutalizes him. Moreover, it encourages him in his bestiality."[25] Hanes Walton observed:

Dehumanization can play more complex tricks with the psyche than a Christian ethic of love and redemptive suffering can perhaps adequately deal with. . . . Compassion from someone whom you consider beneath you or whom you have harmed is enraging. One can respond to humor, behave justly, and relate to compassion only in situations where justice, compassion and humor are valued. If this is so, then there are only certain circumstances under which people can respond at all, much less compassionately, to their fellow man's suffering.[26]

The attitudes of Laurie Pritchett, Bull Connor, Jim Clark, after their experiences with the nonviolent resisters, substantiate the conclusions of Killens and Walton about King's concept of redemptive suffering. Pritchett, Connor, and Clark still had the same contempt for blacks after their communities came under nonviolent siege as they had before. Their prejudice, their hatred, their resentments toward black Americans were neither lessened nor abated. When people feel that their way of life is being challenged, they do not visualize their actions as brutal but as appropriate in protecting and holding intact that which they regard as sacrosanct. In the minds of the defenders of the status quo, those who are injured in the process only receive their just due for "getting out of their place."

King, however, remained firmly convinced that unearned suffering used creatively could effect social change. His commitment was one which had evolved out of the crucible of his own trials and suffering. By the time *Strength to Love* was written, he had been imprisoned in Alabama and Georgia twelve times. His home had been bombed twice, and he had been the victim of a near fatal stabbing. As his sufferings increased, he realized that he could respond in one of two ways. He could react with bitterness, or he could seek to transform his suffering into a creative force. King chose the latter course by attempting to make a virtue out of suffering. The approach personally convinced him of the value of creative suffering. He wrote:

I have lived these last few years with the conviction that unearned suffering is redemptive. There are some who still find the Cross a stumbling block, others consider it foolishness, but I am more convinced than ever before that it is the power of God unto social and individual salvation. So like the Apostle Paul I can now humbly, yet proudly, say, "I bear in my body the marks of the Lord Jesus."[27]

Agape

At the center of King's nonviolent philosophy stands the principle of love. This fifth principle implies that the nonviolent resister must avoid external physical violence and internal violence of the spirit. The nonviolent resister should not only refuse to shoot his adversary but also refuse to hate the adversary. This can be done only when the love ethic is projected to the center of one's life.

When King spoke of love, he did not mean sentimentality or affectionate emotion. He knew that it was neither feasible nor possible to expect the oppressed to love the oppressor in an affectionate sense. King identified the love ethic with the New Testament concept of *agape*. King defined *agape* as "understanding, redeeming good will for all men." It was a purely spontaneous, unmotivated, groundless, and creative, overflowing love. It was not set in motion by any quality or function of its objects but was the love of God operating in the human heart.

Agape, for King, was a disinterested love in which the individual sought not only individual good but also the good of the others. It was entirely a "neighbor-regarding concern for others," which made no distinctions between worthy and unworthy people nor between friend and enemy, but which sought the neighbor in every person it met. King felt that the best way to assure disinterested love was to love the enemy-neighbor from whom one could expect only hostility and persecution in return. *Agape*, for King, also sprang from the need of the other person. God demonstrated *agape* because the act of redemption occurred "while we were yet sinners," at the point of humanity's greatest need for love. Whites need the love of blacks because of the way that segregation has distorted the personalities and scarred the souls of members of the majority community. Blacks exemplify *agape* when they respond to that need by loving those whites who oppose them. King conceptualized *agape* as an active love that sought not only to preserve or to create community but also to restore community. King understood the cross as "the eternal expression of the length to which God will go in order to restore broken community. The resurrection [was the] symbol of God's triumph over all the forces that seek to block community. The Holy Spirit is the continuing community creating reality that moves through history."[28] Therefore, to work against community is to work against the whole of creation. In agreement with the evangelical liberal tradition, King concluded that in the final analysis *agape* meant a recognition of the fact that all of life is interrelated and that all persons are members of the same family to the degree that one cannot harm another without hurting oneself. To demonstrate his point, King observed:

> White men often refuse federal aid to education in order to avoid giving the Negro his rights; but because all men are brothers they cannot deny Negro children without harming their own. They end, all efforts to the contrary, by hurting themselves. Why is this? Because all men are brothers. If you harm me, you harm yourself.[29]

Although King defined *agape* as a selfless and disinterested love, there were, nevertheless, self-interested and egoistic elements in his ethic. His love ethic was not entirely selfless and disinterested. He did seek something in return: equality, freedom, and personal dignity. Although the goals of King's nonviolent ethic were honorable and praiseworthy, the fact remains that his *agape* was neither altogether disinterested nor totally devoted to the well-being of others. The faithful adherence to King's ethic may have had redemptive possibilities for the neighbor in the long run, and genuine concern for the neighbor may have been integral to its application in various contexts. However, King's ethic was never totally and solely devoted to the well-being of the neighbor with no concern for self.

Of course one wonders if *agape* can be realized fully by or in human beings in history. According to thinkers such as Niebuhr, *agape* operating in the human heart can never be purged of all of its egoistic and self-interested elements. Even the purest form of *agape*, the love of the enemy and the forgiveness of the enemy's evil, does not exist apart from the limitations and pitfalls of historical existence. The only *agape*, symbolized by the cross, that is capable of being totally disinterested and selfless is the *agape* of God. Hanes Walton questioned the capacity and the capability of men and women to express, in their historical setting, the *agape* as conceptualized by King. Walton wrote:

> It is questionable whether the ordinary person is capable of achieving the *agape* level of love. Can modern men, characteristically self-centered and aggressive, overcome the qualities and attain the transcendent love symbolized by Christ on the cross? . . . . How realistic

is it to expect of people united for basically political purposes a standard of love normally out of reach of all but the most singular among men?[30]

King was aware of the difficulty of practicing *agape* and thus his language, like much of the language of theology, is a statement of an ideal for which he strived rather than a testimony of the perfection that he had attained. He was acutely aware of the egoistic elements within his own heart as well as the hearts of others. This is why he understood *agape* as the power of God operating within the human heart. It is the power of God rather than human intuition that makes *agape* conceivable, operable, and potentially attainable.

Many questioned King's belief that love is necessary for the most effective use of a nonviolent method of resisting injustice. Many civil rights organizations, labor unions, and other groups devoted to any number of causes have used nonviolence with excellent results—without emphasizing love as a "regulating ideal." Concrete measures such as court injunctions, boycotts, picket lines, mass demonstrations, strikes, sit-ins, lie-ins, and other tactics have succeeded quite independently of either the presence or absence of love as a factor. While it is desirable that nonviolent resisters, for the sake of effectiveness and beneficial long-term consequences, minimize their hostility and maximize their goodwill for their opponent, the emphasis on love is still a "helpful refinement" rather than a requirement for nonviolent action. When love is interpreted as a requirement for nonviolence, persons who have been victims of acts of cruelty by their oppressors and who are unable to love them may turn toward violence as the technique most consistent with their resentment and hostilities. One analyst has written:

> This confusion of secondary refinements with primary requirements and alienation of many potential users of the nonviolent technique has sometimes been aggravated by attempts of pacifists and believers in the principles of nonviolence to proselytize within nonviolent action movements, and to blur the distinctions between their beliefs and the nonviolent technique. Such efforts may in the long run impede rather than promote the substitution of nonviolent for violent means.[31]

King was aware that his emphasis on love presented as many problems for some of his nonviolent practitioners as did nonviolence itself for a number of black Americans. However, King remained devoted to a ministry of reconciliation with justice, and the creation of the beloved community. Throughout his life King insisted that love was the only force capable of transforming an enemy into a friend. He wrote: "We never get rid of an enemy by meeting hate with hate; we get rid of an enemy by getting rid of enmity. By its very nature, hate destroys and tears down; by its very nature, love creates and builds up. Love tranforms with redemptive power."[32]

The Universe as an Ally of Justice

The sixth principle of King's nonviolent philosophy reflects the influence of evangelical liberalism upon his thinking. This principle is the conviction that the universe is on the side of justice. This conviction gives the nonviolent resister faith in the future and strength to accept suffering without retaliation.

King recognized that all nonviolent practitioners may not ascribe to his belief in a personal God. He maintained, nevertheless, that even these persons believe in some kind of creative force which works for "universal wholeness." He stated that "whether we call it an unconscious process, an impersonal Brahman, or a Personal Being of matchless power and infinite love, there is a creative force in this universe that works to bring the disconnected aspect of reality into a harmonious whole."[33]

As has been noted, King's belief in nonviolence was grounded in his faith in God. Although other significant nonviolent theorists and practitioners have also affirmed the existence of a higher being or creative force, it would be an error to conclude that nonviolence presupposes theism. Although historically theism has been related to nonviolence as well as to violence, there is no logical sequence or inevitability that requires a theistic premise either for the endorsement of violence or a commitment to nonviolence. Humanists and atheists, as well as theists, may be committed to nonviolence both as a method for social change and as a way of life. A person's commitment to nonviolence may be grounded in the social or political struggle in which one is engaged. Just as there is no inevitability between the adoption of nonviolence as a strategy and the adoption of nonviolence as a way of life, there is no inevitability between nonviolence and theism. Nonviolence may or may not be grounded in theism.

King's belief that the universe is on the side of justice cannot be proved or disproved. One's conclusions about the ultimate meaning of the universe and about life itself depends upon one's perspective and orientation. King spoke and wrote from the perspective of religious faith. The writer of the Letter to the Hebrews has stated that "faith is the assurance of things hoped for, the conviction of things not seen" (11:1, RSV). In the final analysis, matters of faith cannot be proved or disproved—either they are believed or they are not.

When King was killed by a bullet from a sniper's rifle, some persons viewed his death as tragic. Others commented that it was ironic that a person whose life was committed to nonviolence died by violence. Still others felt that King's violent death was a refutation of his philosophy and a demonstration of the failure of his nonviolent methodology. King, however, as a man of faith, looked toward his death as redemptive. In *Stride Toward Freedom* he made a statement that he would repeat over and over again in the years ahead: "If physical death is the price that a man must pay to free his children and his white brethren from a permanent death of the spirit, then nothing could be more redemptive."[34]

Martin Luther King, Jr., the man of faith, believed in his God. On the night preceding his death, it was his faith in God that empowered him to declare with renewed strength his conviction that black people would inevitably and assuredly triumph. His words still hold hope:

> We've got some difficult days ahead. But it really doesn't matter to me now. Because I've been to the mountaintop. . . .
>
> Like anybody else, I would like to live a long life. Longevity has its place. But I'm not concerned about that now. I just want to do God's will. And He's allowed me to go up to the mountain. And I've looked over, and I've seen the Promised Land.
>
> I may not get there with you, but I want you to know tonight that we as a people will get to the Promised Land.
>
> So I'm happy tonight. I'm not worried about anything. I'm not fearing any man. Mine eyes have seen the glory of the coming of the Lord.[35]

Conclusion

W hat are the implications of Martin King's non-violent ethic for persons who are engaged in life-and-death battles with principalities and powers, with the rulers of darkness, with spiritual hosts of wickedness in high places? One of the primary lessons that Christians with a sense of social consciousness can glean from King's ethical style is this: oppression and evil must be resisted. Whenever and wherever injustice exists, whatever the form—be it racial, economic, or political—it must be resisted. If King is used as a paradigm for Christian resistance, one could further assert that the basic rationale for Christian resistance must be theological and that the means must be ethically consistent with the ends. The Christian may use other frames of reference, such as the law, to legitimate his or her claims or behavior. There may be instances when the Christian may even argue from a pragmatic point of view. However, the predominant standard for the Christian, with which all other frames of reference must be consistent and against which behavior or actions are mea-sured, is theological.

Martin Luther King, Jr., was essentially a moral theorist. The frame of reference from which he functioned, from which he viewed life and the world in all of its facets and aspects, and from which he made his ethical decisions was not what was merely politically expedient. Neither was it totally dependent upon the exigencies of the situation. Instead, it was what he considered to be morally right or wrong. King viewed as moral that which was in accord with the eternal and abiding principles of the Christian faith. Immorality was whatever existed in dissonance to the eternal and divine principles of the Christian faith. To understand King as a man, as a leader, or as a thinker or to understand his nonviolent ethic, one ought to consider him as a man of faith who subscribed to certain irrefutable and irrevocable moral laws.

King stated that "moral ends" ought to be pursued by "moral means." One must be careful, however, about the definition of "moral means." Nonviolence for King was the "morally excellent way." He viewed violence as not only impractical but also immoral. Christians, however, ought never forget that the crucifixion of Jesus Christ, which many regard as the central act in the redemption of humanity, was a violent occurrence. While it is true that the violence was not responsible for the redemption of humanity, it is also true that a violent act was an integral part of the process of redemption. In a similar vein, it can be stated that violence was an extremely important factor in the programming and application of King's nonviolent method. King was well aware of the utilitarian advantages of violence for a nonviolent methodology and he exploited them well. King's greatest successes occurred in those campaigns in which King's protesters were met by a violent response that generated public support. Nonviolence was less effective in those instances in which there was no violent response to marshal public opinion in support of the nonviolent resisters. Even the threat of violence was a means of persuasion in negotiations.

Even though he condemned and rejected it, violence, ironically, played a peculiarly supportive role for King's nonviolent method. One must be careful, then, about ascribing morality to one's means. Social struggles are so complex that one's means are seldom as pure as one might suppose. The struggle for justice, when carved in a special social and political setting, is not always a matter of black and white, of totally nonviolent or totally violent means. There are a number of gray areas in which the Christian must move with caution and flexibility. Consequently, one must be sure that one's definition of "moral means" is broad enough for some degree of flexibility. At times the rigidity of King's ethical style and the singularity of his approach were liabilities when he moved to new terrain. Openness in the selection of the most effective means to bring justice to a particular situation does not necessarily do violence to the commitment to maintain the sacred relationship between means and ends. Flexibility is necessary when one is dealing with an adversary whose mind-set and whose priorities are different from one's own. A posture of flexibility with regard to the specific means for a particular situation is a risky stance. Max Weber has observed: "No ethics in the world can dodge the fact that in numerous instances the attainment of 'good' ends is bound to the fact that one must be willing to pay the price of using morally dubious means or at least dangerous ones—and facing the possibility of evil ramifications."[1]

There is no way to advance the cause of justice other than by taking risks on one's convictions or one's beliefs or one's God. There are no guarantees for success and there are no hedges against failure. Without hearing any special voice, seeing any special visions, or directly receiving any special revelation, Christians must often make judgments and reach decisions that are in accord with those principles that they believe with all their hearts, souls, and minds, in the hope that time and history will prove that they acted on behalf of justice. In situations in which there are no clear indications regarding the direction that one ought to go, the Christian response is based not only upon what can be deduced logically but also upon what is felt, sensed, and believed from within. The hope is that undergirded by the power of God, by the temerity of one's witness, and by the integrity of one's ethical style, one can facilitate positive social changes.

It is the hope and the belief of socially conscious Christians and other socially sensitive persons that they can make a difference in the plight of humankind. If Martin Luther King, Jr., and his nonviolent ethic proved anything, it was that individuals—without guarantees of success and in spite of their failures, weaknesses, and limitations—can make a difference. Its limitations notwithstanding, nonviolence as understood and interpreted by King was, nevertheless, an effective strategy and ethic. As King's ethic is critiqued, one must never forget that his nonviolent ethic evolved out of situations of crisis.

Although King knew about Gandhi's work and believed that nonviolence had potential as a viable strategy for the oppressed, he had not given serious thought to the formulation of a Christian ethic of nonviolence until he became involved in the Montgomery bus boycott. The organization, the codification, and the integration of the various strands of evangelical liberalism and personalism into the nucleus of a nonviolent social ethic was a process that happened soon after the arrest of Rosa Parks. Although it was undergirded by a distinct theological perspective, King's ethic, from its inception, was intended to be an applied ethic. Its theological foundation provided it with its intellectual framework and rationale, as it attempted to respond to the various crises and provide answers to the various ethical dilemmas encountered in black America's quest for freedom and equality. Its theological foundation gave a needed stability to King's ethic as well as room for growth when those crisis situations and dilemmas demanded flexibility, a revision of goals, and a restructure of priorities. King's ethic was subjected to some of the most rugged criteria for its validation. It was judged by its effectiveness in the situation. Martin King, then, was no armchair philosopher or ethicist. Part of the significance of King's ethic was that it was not only social theory but also social action. Much of King's significance as an ethicist is found not in the originality of his thinking but in his attempts to apply in creative ways the tenets of his faith and his ethic to situations of social conflict.

. The role of social theoretician, however, was not the basic vocation of Martin Luther King, Jr. When the Montgomery bus boycott began, King was essentially an exceptionally well-educated pastor in a Baptist church. He was engaged in those routines normally associated with shepherding the flock. He was a local leader who tried to apply his experience and Christian beliefs to the resolution of a local conflict. The Christian label was not meant to be exclusionary but indicative of the source, the *weltanschauung*, as well as the theology or faith perspective of the nonviolent practitioners. In the Southern Bible belt that furnished the original arena for the application of King's nonviolent ethic and among the church people who formed his initial constituency, the Christian emphasis was more inclusive than exclusive. A Christian ethic in Montgomery, Alabama, in the mid-1950s had broader mass appeal and commanded more respect than any other ethic. When King attempted to secure from his followers a commitment to nonviolence that was akin to religious conversion (or one that was made with the heart as well as with the head), he simply reflected the basic style of the preacher that he was, who Sunday after Sunday mounted his pulpit and called "sinners to repentance."

Martin King was a doctor of philosophy in the theological tradition of evangelical liberalism. He was also a social activist and Nobel Peace Prize winner. Although his perspective had been broadened by his exposure to a number of ideas, persons, and experiences, throughout his life Martin Luther King, Jr., remained fundamentally and essentially a black Christian preacher. More than Gandhism, or Boston personalism, or the evangelical liberalism of Crozer Theological Seminary, it was black religion that gave King his distinctiveness among leaders. Nurtured in its bosom, he embraced the rhythmic style of its preaching, the theological perspective of its spirituals, and much of its piety.

During the early days of the bus boycott when there was no consciousness of Gandhism on the part of the leaders, there was an awareness of Christian principles—specifically the love ethic of Jesus, as understood and articulated by the black preacher through the black church. The black Christian church perspective had its limitations, as does every perspective. No perspective can be all things to all people. No perspective is broad enough to appeal to all people in all places at all times. A perspective by its very nature limits and defines its constituency. King's perspective defined not only his constituency but also him. At times the personal religious belief, the black church tradition, and the Christian theology that helped King to understand and articulate the meaning of his faith may have seemed to limit his appeal and the implication of some of his more activist views. However, these elements were also the source of King's inner strength. Without them he would not have been the charismatic personality or the unique leader of humanity that he was.

When one reads King's writings or listens to his various re-
cordings, one notes how thoroughly imbued they are with hope.
Although experience helped him grow beyond his early naivete
and though reality tempered his optimism, hope remained an
essential ingredient of his ethical consciousness. Through all the
changes that his life and thinking underwent, King never ceased
to hope. Even when America had demonstrated time and time
again that it had no intention of changing its attitude regarding
the liberation of blacks and all who are oppressed (until or unless
it was forced to do so), King continued to talk about its redemption. If King could love to the end, it was because he could
hope to the end, for where there is no hope, there is no love.
Perhaps one of the black church's most endearing and enduring
gifts to King was hope. Whenever one examines the literature
and participates in the oral tradition of black religion, one sees
that, historically, black people have been persistently hopeful.

Some label this insistence on "a bright side somewhere" as
eschatology, possibly realized but probably final. To others it is
an opiate, a pie in the sky. Black people, however, know the
force that energizes their tired beings and forces them to "keep
on keeping on," even when stress tests and data about human
endurance tell them that they should have given out and given
up long ago—that force is hope. Black people know the power
that causes them, during the most difficult periods of their history, to mount up with wings like eagles, to run and not be
weary, to walk and not faint—that power is hope. When oppression has crushed their aspirations and their dreams have been
dashed against the hard rock of racism, black people know what
has helped them to pick up the pieces and dare to dream again—
it is hope. Black people have always understood the message of
Paul when he wrote that ". . . suffering produces endurance,
and endurance produces character, and character produces hope,
and hope does not disappoint us, because God's love has been
poured into our hearts through the Holy Spirit which has been
given to us" (Romans 5:3-5, RSV).

Martin Luther King, Jr., was heir to this hope and it is what
kept him going when he saw his dreams deferred after many
trials and numerous disappointments. From the vantage point
of a matured perspective and concern for those issues that had
occupied his thinking during the later years of his life, King, in

The Trumpet of Conscience, still talked about his dream. He said:

Yes, I am personally the victim of deferred dreams, of blasted hopes, but in spite of that I close today by saying I still have a dream, because, you know, you can't give up in life. If you lose hope, somehow you lose that vitality that keeps life moving, you lose courage to be, that quality that helps you go on in spite of all. And so today I still have a dream.

I have a dream that one day men will rise up and come to see that they are made to live together as brothers. . . . I still have a dream today that one day the idle industries of Appalachia will be revitalized, and the empty stomachs of Mississippi will be filled, and that brotherhood will be more than a few words at the end of a prayer, but rather the first order of business on every legislative agenda. . . . I still have a dream today that one day war will come to an end, that men will beat their swords into ploughshares and their spears into pruning hooks, that nations will no longer rise up against nations, neither will they study war any more. . . . With this faith we will be able to speed up the day when there will be peace on earth and goodwill toward men. It will be a glorious day, the morning stars will sing together, and the sons of God will shout for joy.[2]

Bibliography

Books and Papers by Martin Luther King, Jr.

"A Comparison of the Conceptions of God in the Thinking of Paul Tillich and Henry Nelson Wieman." Unpublished dissertation submitted in partial fulfillment of the requirements for the degree of Doctor of Philosophy, Boston University Graduate School, 1955 (copyright 1958). Ann Arbor, Mich.: University Microfilms, 1968.

Stride Toward Freedom. New York: Harper and Row, Publishers, Inc., 1958.

Strength to Love. New York: Harper and Row, Publishers, Inc., 1963.

Why We Can't Wait. New York: Harper and Row, Publishers, Inc., 1963.

Where Do We Go from Here: Chaos or Community? New York: Harper and Row, Publishers, Inc., 1967.

The Trumpet of Conscience. New York: Harper and Row, Publishers, Inc., 1968.

Selected Writings from the Martin Luther King, Jr., Papers, 1955-61, Boston University Mugar Memorial Library.

Sermons, Speeches, Statements, Letters, and Various Manuscripts by Martin Luther King, Jr.

These materials are available in the Martin Luther King Collection at Boston University. Other sermons and material are available at the Martin Luther King, Jr., Center for Social Change in Atlanta, Ga.

"How My Mind Has Changed in the Last Decade." Article in *Christian Century* (April 7, 1960).

"It Is Finished." Sermon.

"The Nation's Future," NBC Television, November 26, 1960. Text of debate between Martin Luther King, Jr., and James Kilpatrick.

"A Realistic Look at the Question of Progress in the Area of Race Relations." Address delivered at the Second Anniversary of the NAACP Legal Defense and Educational Fund at the Waldorf Astoria Hotel, New York City, May 17, 1956.

"Religious Indecision." Sermon.

Speech delivered at Lincoln Memorial, Washington, D.C., August 28, 1963.

Speech delivered at the Prayer Pilgrimage for Freedom at the Lincoln Memorial, Washington, D.C., May 17, 1957.

Statement at mass meeting in response to the tributes paid him, First Baptist Church, Montgomery, Ala., February 1, 1960.

Statement before the Platform Committee of the Republican National Convention, San Francisco, Calif., July 7, 1964.

Statement concerning endorsement of presidential candidates, November 1, 1960.

Statement of King's call to ministry. Prepared for American Baptist Convention, August 7, 1959.

Essays, Reports, and Research Projects by Martin Luther King, Jr.

"A Conception and Impression of Religion Drawn from Dr. Brightman's Book Entitled *A Philosophy of Religion*"

"The Character of the Christian God"

"How a Christian Overcomes Evil"

"How Modern Christians Should Think of Man"

"Karl Barth's Conception of God"

"The Place of Reason and Experience in Finding God"

"Reinhold Niebuhr"

"Reinhold Niebuhr's Ethical Dualism"

"Religious Answer to the Problem of Evil"

"Six Talks in Outline"
   a. "The Character of the Christian God"
   b. "The Nature of Man"
   c. "Who Was Jesus of Nazareth?"
   d. "What Did Jesus Achieve from His Life and Death?"
   e. "How God Works Today Through His Spirit"
   f. "What Christians Believe About the Church"

"What a Christian Should Believe About Himself"

"What Christians Believe About History and the Future"

Other Related Materials

Davis, George W., "God and History," *Crozer Quarterly*, vol. 20, no. 1 (January 1943), pp. 18-36.

Nelson, William Stuart, "Satyagraha: Gandhian Principles of Non-Violent Non-Cooperation," *The Journal of Religious Thought* (Autumn-Winter, 1957-1958), pp. 15-24.

Selected Articles by Martin Luther King, Jr.

"The Acceptance Speech of Martin Luther King, Jr., of the Nobel Peace Prize on December 10, 1964," *Negro History Bulletin* (May 1968) p. 20.

"America's Racial Crisis," *Current* (May 1968), p. 6-10.

"Advice for Living," *Ebony*, vol. 12, no. 11 (September 1957), p. 74; vol. 12, no. 12 (October 1957), p. 53; vol. 13, no. 2 (December 1957), p. 120; vol. 13, no. 3 (January 1958), p. 34; vol. 13, no. 4 (February 1958), p. 84; vol. 13, no. 5 (March 1958), p. 92; vol. 13, no. 6 (April 1958), p. 104; vol. 13, no. 7 (May

1958), p. 112; vol. 13, no. 9 (July 1958), p. 86; vol. 13, no. 10 (August 1958), p. 78; vol. 13, no. 11 (September 1958), p. 68; vol 13, no. 12 (October 1958), p. 138; vol. 14, no. 1 (November 1958), p. 138; vol 14, no. 2 (December 1958), p. 159.

"Behind the Selma March," *Saturday Review* (April 3, 1965), pp. 16-17.

"Dreams of Brighter Tomorrows," *Ebony*, vol. 20, no. 5 (March 1965), pp. 34-35.

Editorials from the SCLC Newsletter, *Negro History Bulletin* (May 1968), p. 18.

"Equality Now: The President Has the Power," *Nation* (February 4, 1961), pp. 91-95.

"It's a Difficult Thing to Teach a President," *Look* (November 17, 1964), p. 61.

"A Legacy of Creative Protest," *Massachusetts Review* (Autumn 1962), p. 43.

"Love, Law and Civil Disobedience," *New South* (December 1961), pp. 3-11.

"The Luminous Promise," *Progressive* (December 1962), pp. 34-37.

"Non-Violence: The Only Road to Freedom," *Ebony*, vol. 21, no. 12 (October 1966), pp. 27-30.

"Playboy Interview with Martin Luther King," *Playboy* (January 1965), pp. 65-68.

"Role of the Behaviorial Scientist in the Civil Rights Movement," *Journal of Social Issues* (January 1968) pp. 1-12.

"A Testament of Hope," *Playboy* (January 1969), p. 175.

"A Time to Break Silence," *Freedomways* (Spring 1967), pp. 103-117.

"The Un-Christian Christian," *Ebony*, vol. 20, no. 10 (August 1965), pp. 76-80.

"Who Is Their God?" *Nation* (October 13, 1962), pp. 209-210.

Other Selected Writings and Speeches

"Man in a Revolutionary World." Speech from the *Minutes*, Fifth General Synod, United Church of Christ, Chicago, July 1-7, 1965, pp. 236-244.

"Vietnam and the Struggle for Human Rights" (also known as "Time to Break Silence"). Speech delivered at the Riverside Church, New York City, April 4, 1967.

Gregg, Richard B., *In the Power of Nonviolence*. 2nd rev. ed. Foreword. New York: Fellowship Press, 1959, p. 9.

Huie, William Bradford, *Three Lives for Mississippi*. New York: Signet Books, 1965, pp. 8-9.

Lincoln, C. Eric, ed., *Is Anybody Listening to Black America?* New York: The Seabury Press, Inc., 1968. Excerpts from *Where Do We Go From Here?*, the "I Have a Dream" speech, and the "Drum Major for Justice" sermon.

Selected Books About Martin Luther King, Jr.

Ansbro, John J., *Martin Luther King, Jr.: The Making of a Mind*. Maryknoll, N.Y.: Orbis Books, 1982.

Bennett, Lerone, Jr., *What Manner of Man: A Biography of Martin Luther King, Jr.* New York: Pocket Books, 1965.

Bishop, Jim, *The Days of Martin Luther King, Jr.* New York: G. P. Putnam's Sons, 1971.

Clayton, Edward, *Martin Luther King: The Peaceful Warrior*. 3rd ed. Englewood Cliffs, N.J.: Prentice-Hall, Inc., 1970.

Fisher, William H., *Free at Last: A Biography of Martin Luther King, Jr.* Metuchen, N.J.: Scarecrow Press, Inc., 1977.

Garrow, David J., *Protest at Selma: Martin Luther King, Jr. and the Voting Rights Act of 1965*. New Haven: Yale University Press, 1978.

_____, *The FBI and Martin Luther King, Jr.* New York: W. W. Norton & Company, Inc., 1981.

Goodwin, Bennie, *Dr. Martin Luther King, Jr.: God's Messenger of Love, Justice and Hope*. Jersey City: Goodpatrick Publishers, 1976.

Johnson, William, *King*. New York: St. Martin's Press, Inc., 1978.

King, Coretta S., *My Life with Martin Luther King, Jr.* New York: Avon Books, 1970.

Lane, Mark, and Gregory, Dick, *Code Name "Zorro."* Englewood Cliffs, N.J.: Prentice-Hall, Inc., 1978.

Lewis, David L., *King: A Critical Biography*. Baltimore: Penguin Books, 1970.

Lincoln, C. Eric, ed., *Martin Luther King, Jr.: A Profile*. New York: Hill & Wang, 1970.

Lokos, Lionel, *House Divided: The Life and Legacy of Martin Luther King*. New York: Arlington House Publishers, 1968.

Lomax, Louis E., *To Kill a Black Man*. Los Angeles: Holloway House Publishing Co., 1968.

Miller, William R., *Martin Luther King, Jr.: His Life, Martyrdom and Meaning for the World*. New York: Weybright & Talley, Inc., 1968.

Oates, Stephen B., *Let the Trumpet Sound: The Life of Martin Luther King, Jr.* New York: Harper and Row, Publishers, Inc., 1982.

Reddick, L. D., *Crusader Without Violence: A Biography of Martin Luther King, Jr.* New York: Harper and Row, Publishers, Inc., 1959.

Smith, Kenneth L., and Zepp, Ira G., Jr., *Search for the Beloved Community: The Thinking of Martin Luther King, Jr.* Valley Forge: Judson Press, 1974.

Walton, Hanes, Jr., *The Political Philosophy of Martin Luther King, Jr.* Westport, Conn.: Greenwood Press, 1971.

Westin, Alan E. and Mahoney, Barry, *The Trial of Martin Luther King*. New York: Thomas Y. Crowell, 1974.

Williams, John A., *The King God Didn't Save: Reflections on the Life and Death of Martin Luther King, Jr.* New York: Simon and Schuster, 1971.

Selected Articles About Martin Luther King, Jr.

"Accident in Harlem," *Time* (September 29, 1958), p. 14.

"An American Tragedy: State Troopers Charge Marching Negroes at Selma, Alabama," *Newsweek*, (March 22, 1965), pp. 18-21.

Barrett, George, "Jim Crow, He's Real Tired," *New York Times Magazine* (March 3, 1957), p. 11.

——————, "Montgomery: Testing Ground," *New York Times Magazine* (December 16, 1956), pp. 8-9.

Bennett, Lerone, Jr., "From Booker T. to Martin L.," *Ebony* (November 1962), pp. 152-162.

——————, "The King Plan for Freedom," *Ebony* (July 1956), pp. 65-69. Reprinted in *Ebony* (November 1975), pp. 91-93.

——————, and Allan Morrison, "The South and the Negro," *Ebony* (April 1957), p. 77.

"The Big Man Is Martin Luther King, Jr.," *Newsweek* (July 29, 1963), pp. 30-32.

Booker, Simeon, "50,000 March on Montgomery," *Ebony* (May 1965), pp. 46-48.

Dunbar, Ernest, "A Visit with Martin Luther King," *Look* (February 12, 1963), pp. 92-96.

Elder, John D., "Martin Luther King and American Civil Religion," *Harvard Divinity School Bulletin* (Spring 1968), pp. 17-18.

Garber, Paul, "King Was a Theologian," *The Journal of Religious Thought*, vol. 21, no. 2 (Fall-Winter 1974-75).

Halberstam, David, "Notes from the Bottom of the Mountain," *Harper's Bazaar* (June 1968), pp. 40-42.

Hanigan, James P., "Martin Luther King, Jr.: The Images of a Man," *The Journal of Political Thought*, vol. 21, no. 1 (Spring-Summer 1974).

"Is It Right to Break the Law?" *U.S. News and World Report* (August 12, 1963), p. 6.

The Journal of the Interdenominational Theological Center, vol. 3, no. 2 (Spring 1976).

  Dewolf, L. Harold, "Martin Luther King, Jr., as Theologian" pp. 1-11.

  Hoyt, Thomas, Jr., "The Biblical Tradition of the Poor and

Martin Luther King, Jr.," pp. 12-32.

Oglesby, Enoch, H., "Martin Luther King Jr., Liberation Ethics in a Christian Context," pp. 33-47.

Turner, Otis, "Nonviolence and the Politics of Liberation," pp. 49-60.

Morres, Calvin, "Martin Luther King, Jr., Exemplary Preacher," pp. 61-66.

"King Moves North," *Time* (April 30, 1965), pp. 32-33.

"King's Last Tape," *Newsweek* (December 16, 1968), p. 34.

Maguire, John David, "Martin Luther King and Vietnam," *Christianity and Crisis*, vol. 27, no. 7 (May 1967)

McKinney, Richard I, "The Ethics of Dissent," *The Journal of Religious Thought*, vol. 29, no. 2 (Autumn-Winter 1972).

Meier, August, "On the Role of Martin Luther King," *New Politics* (Winter 1965), pp. 52-59.

Quarles, Benjamin, "Martin Luther King in History," *Negro History Bulletin* (May 1968), p. 9.

Sanders, Charles L., "The Tortuous Road to Oslo," *Ebony* (March 1965), p. 36.

Sellers, James E., "Love, Justice, and the Non-violent Movement," *Theology Today* (January 1962), pp. 422-434.

Smith, Donald H., "An Exegesis of Martin Luther King's Social Philosophy," *Phylon* (Spring 1970), pp. 89-97.

Smith, Lillian, "And Suddenly Something Happened," *Saturday Review* (September 20, 1958), p. 21.

Steinkraus, Warren E., "Martin Luther King's Personalism and Nonviolence," *Journal of the History of Ideas* (January 1973), pp. 97-111.

"Still King," *Christian Century* (September 7, 1966), p. 1071.

"Surfeit of Surveillance," *Christian Century* (July 9, 1969), p. 917.

"Transcendent Symbol," *Time* (April 12, 1968), pp 19-21.

Willis, Gary, "Martin Luther King Is Still on the Case!" *Esquire* (August 1968), pp. 98-104.

Radio and Television Transcripts

WNET, Bill Moyers Journal, April 2, 1979, "Andrew Young Remembers Martin Luther King."

Other Selected Books

Andrews, C. F., *Mahatma Gandhi's Ideas*. New York: Macmillan Inc., 1930.

──────, ed., *Mahatma Gandhi—His Own Story*. New York: Macmillan Inc., 1930.

──────, ed., *Mahatma Gandhi at Work—His Own Story Continued*. New York: Macmillan Inc., 1931.

Arendt, Hannah, *On Violence*. New York: Harcourt Brace Jovanovich Inc., 1969.

Bainton, Roland H., *Christian Attitudes Toward War and Peace*. Nashville: Abingdon Press, 1960.

Bedau, Hugo Adam, *Civil Disobedience: Theory and Practice*. New York: Pegasus, 1969.

Bennett, Lerone, *The Negro Mood*. Boulder, Colo.: Johnson Publishing Company, 1969.

Bianchi, Eugene C., *The Religious Experience of Revolutionaries*. Garden City, N.Y.: Doubleday and Company, Inc., 1962.

Boesak, Allan Aubrey, *Farewell to Innocence*. Maryknoll, N.Y.: Orbis Books, 1977.

Bonhoeffer, Dietrich, *The Cost of Discipleship*. New York: Macmillan Inc., 1937 (1970).

──────, *Ethics*. New York: Macmillan Inc., 1949 (1969).

Boulware, Marcus H., *The Oratory of Negro Leaders: 1900-1968*. Westport, Conn.: Negro Universities Press, 1969.

Brown, Robert McAfee, *Religion and Violence*. Philadelphia: The Westminster Press, 1973.

Carmichael, Stokeley, and Hamilton, Charles V., *Black Power: The Politics of Liberation in America*. New York: Vintage Books, division of Random House, 1968.

Cleage, Albert B., Jr., *The Black Messiah*. New York: Sheed and

Ward, 1968.

Cleaver, Eldridge, *Soul on Ice*. New York: McGraw-Hill, Inc., 1968.

Cone, James, *Black Theology and Black Power*. New York: The Seabury Press, Inc., 1969.

_____, *A Black Theology of Liberation*. New York: J. B. Lippincott Co., 1970.

Crotty, William J., ed., *Assassinations and the Political Order*. New York: Harper and Row, Publishers, Inc. 1971.

Cruse, Harold, *Rebellion or Revolution*. New York: William Morrow and Company, Inc., 1968.

DuBois, W. E. Burghardt, *The Souls of Black Folk*. New York: The New American Library, Inc., 1969.

Ellul, Jacques, *Violence: Reflections from a Christian Perspective*. New York: The Seabury Press, Inc., 1969.

Erikson, Erik H., *Gandhi's Truth*. New York: W. W. Norton and Company, Inc., 1969.

Fager, Charles R., *Selma 1965: The Town Where the South Was Changed*. New York: Charles Scribner's Sons, 1974.

_____, *Uncertain Resurrection: The Poor People's Washington Campaign*. Grand Rapids: William B. Eerdmans Publishing Company, 1969.

Fanon, Frantz, *The Wretched of the Earth*. New York: Grove Press, Inc., 1968.

Foner, Philip S., ed., *The Voice of Black America*. New York: Simon and Schuster, 1972.

Gandhi, Mohandas K. *An Autobiography: Or the Story of My Experiments with Truth*. Boston: Beacon Press, 1957.

Gandhi, Mohandas K. *Non-Violent Resistance*. New York: Schocken Books, Inc., 1961.

Gerth, Hans H., and Mills, C. Wright, trs. *From Max Weber: Essays in Sociology*. New York: Oxford University Press, Inc., 1946.

Grant, Joanne, ed., *Black Protest: History, Documents and Analyses from 1619 to the Present*. New York: Fawcett Books Group, 1968.

Hall, Robert T., *The Morality of Civil Disobedience*. New York: Harper Torchbooks, Harper and Row, Publishers, Inc., 1971.

Hamilton, Charles, *The Black Preacher in America*. New York: William Morrow and Company, Inc., 1972.

Harvey, Van A., *A Handbook of Theological Terms*. New York: Macmillan Inc., 1964.

Hofstadter, Richard, and Wallace, Michael, eds., *American Violence: A Documentary History*. New York: Alfred A. Knopf, Inc., 1970.

Hordern, William, *A Layman's Guide to Protestant Theology*. New York: Macmillan Inc., 1955.

Huie, William B., *He Slew the Dreamer: My Search for the Truth About James Earl Ray and the Murder of Martin Luther King*. New York: Delacorte Press, 1968.

Jones, Major, *Christian Ethics for Black Theology*. Nashville: Abingdon Press, 1974.

Kegley, Charles W., and Bretall, Robert W., *Reinhold Niebuhr: His Religious, Social and Political Thought*. New York: Macmillan Inc., 1962.

King, Martin Luther, Sr., and Riley, Clayton, *Daddy King: The Autobiography of Martin Luther King, Sr.* New York: William Morrow and Company, Inc., 1980.

Lincoln, C. Eric, *The Black Church Since Frazier*. New York: Schocken Books, Inc., 1974.

———, *Sounds of the Struggle: Persons and Perspectives in Civil Rights*. New York: William Morrow and Company, Inc., 1971.

———, ed., *The Black Experience in Religion: A Collection of Readings*. New York: Doubleday and Company, Inc., 1974.

Lomax, Louis E., *The Negro Revolt*. New York: Harper and Row, Publishers, Inc., 1962.

Long, Edward Leroy, Jr., *War and Conscience in America*. Philadelphia: The Westminster Press, 1978.

Lynd, Staughton, ed., *Nonviolence in America: A Documentary History*. Indianapolis: The Bobbs-Merrill Company, Inc., 1965.

Macgregor, G. H. C., *The New Testament Basis of Pacifism and the Relevance of an Impossible Ideal*. New York: Fellowship Publication, 1960.

Malcolm X, *The Autobiography of Malcolm X*. New York: Grove Press, Inc., 1965.

_____, *Malcolm X Speaks*. New York: Grove Press, Inc., 1965.

Marty, Martin E., and Peerman, Dean G., eds., *New Theology*, vol. 6. New York: Macmillan Inc., 1969.

Mays, Benjamin, *Born to Rebel*. New York: Charles Scribner's Sons, 1971.

Meier, August, and Rudwick, Elliott, *Black Protest in the Sixties*. New York: Times Books Quadrangle, 1970.

Meredith, James, *Three Years in Mississippi*. Bloomington: Indiana University Press, 1966.

Miller, William Robert, ed., *Contemporary American Protestant Thought: 1900-1970*. New York: Bobbs-Merrill Company, Inc., 1973.

_____, *Nonviolence: A Christian Interpretation*. New York: Association Press, 1964.

Morris, Colin, *Unyoung, Uncolored, Unpoor*. Nashville: Abingdon Press, 1970.

Merton, Thomas, ed., *Gandhi on Non-Violence*. New York: New Directions Publishing Corp., 1965.

Muse, Benjamin, *The American Negro Revolution from Nonviolence to Black Power 1963-1967*. Bloomington: Indiana University Press, 1968.

Niebuhr, Reinhold, *An Interpretation of Christian Ethics*. New York: Meridian Books, 1956.

_____, *Moral Man and Immoral Society*. New York: Charles Scribner's Sons, 1932 (1960).

_____, *The Nature and Destiny of Man*, vol 1. New York: Charles Scribner's Sons, 1941 (1964).

_____, *The Nature and Destiny of Man*, vol. 2. New York: Charles Scribner's Sons, 1943 (1964).

_____, *Pious and Secular America*. New York: Charles Scribner's Sons, 1958.

Ramachandran, G., and Mahadevan, T. K., ed., *Gandhi: His Relevance for our Times*. New Delhi: Gandhi Peace Foundation, 1967.

Rauschenbusch, Walter, *Christianity and the Social Crisis*. New York: Harper and Row, Publishers, Inc., 1964.

Schlissel, Lillian, ed., *Conscience in America: A Documentary History of Conscientious Objection in America, 1757-1967*. New York: E. P. Dutton, Inc., 1968.

Sharpe, Dores Robinson, *Walter Rauschenbusch*. New York: Macmillan Inc., 1942.

Sharp, Gene, *The Politics of Nonviolent Action*. Boston: Porter Sargent Publishers, Inc., 1974.

Shinn, Roger, *Tangled World*. New York: Charles Scribner's Sons, 1965.

_____, *Wars and Rumors of Wars*. Nashville: Abingdon Press, 1972.

Silberman, Charles E., *Crisis in Black and White*. New York: Random House, Inc., 1964.

Sloan, Irving, Jr., *Our Violent Past: An American Chronicle*. New York: Random House, Inc., 1970.

Swomley, John, Jr., *Liberation Ethics*. New York: Macmillan Inc., 1972.

Washington, Joseph R., Jr., *Black Religion: The Negro and Christianity in the United States*. Boston: Beacon Press, 1964.

_____, *The Politics of God: The Future of the Black Churches*. Boston: Beacon Press, 1967.

Wilmore, Gayraud, *Black Religion and Black Radicalism*. New York: Doubleday and Company, Inc., 1973.

Yoder, John, *Nevertheless*. Scottdale, Pa.: Herald Press, 1972.

_____, *The Politics of Jesus*. Grand Rapids: William B. Eerdmans Publishing Company, 1972.

Zinn, Howard, *SNCC: The New Abolitionists*. Boston: Beacon Press, 1965.

Other Selected Articles

"Ephesians," *The Interpreter's Bible,* vol. 10. Nashville: Abingdon Press, 1953, pp. 597-749.

"The FBI and Civil Rights: J. Edgar Hoover Speaks Out," *U.S. News and World Report* (November 30, 1964), pp. 56-58.

"Playboy Interview: James Earl Ray," *Playboy,* vol. 24, no. 9 (September 1971), pp. 69-81.

"The Use of Martyrdom," *Saturday Review* (April 17, 1968), pp. 28-29.

"Violence, Nonviolence and the Struggle for Social Justice," *Ecumenical Review,* vol. 25, no. 4 (October 1973), pp. 3-19.

Notes

Introduction

[1] "Ephesians," *The Interpreter's Bible*, vol. 10 (Nashville: Abingdon Press, 1953), p. 738.

[2] John Yoder, *The Politics of Jesus* (Grand Rapids: William B. Eerdmans Publishing Company, 1972), p. 152.

[3] "Violence, Nonviolence and the Struggle for Social Justice," *Ecumenical Review*, vol. 25, no. 4 (October, 1973), p. 7.

[4] Herbert Richardson, "Martin Luther King—Unsung Theologian," *New Theology*, vol. 6, ed. Martin E. Marty and Dean G. Peerman (New York: Macmillan Inc., 1969), p. 181.

Chapter 1

[1] L. D. Reddick, *Crusader Without Violence* (New York: Harper and Row, Publishers, Inc., 1959), p. 78, as quoted in Kenneth L. Smith and Ira G. Zepp, Jr., *Search for the Beloved Community: The Thinking of Martin Luther King, Jr.* (Valley Forge: Judson Press, 1974), p. 21.

[2] Kenneth L. Smith and Ira G. Zepp, Jr. *Search for the Beloved Community: The Thinking of Martin Luther King, Jr.* (Valley Forge: Judson Press, 1974), p. 21.

[3] Kenneth Cauthen, *The Impact of American Religious Liberalism* (New York: Harper and Row, Publishers, Inc., 1962), pp. 27, 29, quoted in Smith and Zepp, p. 19.

[4] *Ibid.*

[5] *Ibid.*

[6] Smith and Zepp, *Search for the Beloved Community*, p. 19.

[7] See *ibid.*, pp. 24-28.

[8] George W. Davis, "God and History," *Crozer Quarterly*, vol. 20, no. 1 (January

1943), pp. 21, 35. Reprinted with permission of Colgate Rochester/Bexley Hall/Crozer Divinity School.

⁹Martin Luther King, Jr., *Strength to Love* (New York: Harper and Row, Publishers, Inc., 1963), p. 53.

¹⁰*Ibid.*, p. 72.

¹¹*Ibid.*, pp. 128-129.

¹²Davis, "God and History," p. 36.

¹³Martin Luther King, Jr., *Stride Toward Freedom: The Montgomery Story* (New York: Harper and Row, Publishers, Inc., 1958), pp. 51-52.

¹⁴King, *Strength to Love*, p. 78.

¹⁵*Ibid.*, p. 77.

¹⁶Davis, "God and History," p. 27.

¹⁷*Ibid.*, pp. 28-29.

¹⁸King, *Strength to Love*, pp. 65-66.

¹⁹*Ibid.*

²⁰Martin Luther King, Jr., "What a Christian Should Believe About Himself," Martin Luther King's Papers (Boston, Mass.: Boston University).

²¹Martin Luther King, Jr., *The Trumpet of Conscience* (New York: Harper and Row, Publishers, Inc., 1968), p. 68.

²²David L. Lewis, *King: A Critical Biography* (New York: Penguin Books, 1970), p. 11.

²³Lerone Bennett, *What Manner of Man: A Biography of Martin Luther King, Jr.* (New York: Pocket Books, 1968), p. 25.

²⁴Malcolm X, *The Autobiography of Malcolm X* (New York: Grove Press, Inc., 1965), p. 284.

²⁵Davis, p. 25.

²⁶*Ibid.*

²⁷Quoted in *ibid.*

²⁸King, *Stride Toward Freedom*, p. 82.

²⁹Smith and Zepp, *Search for the Beloved Community*, p. 103.

³⁰King, *Strength to Love*, p. 160.

³¹King, *Stride Toward Freedom*, p. 75.

³²Smith and Zepp, *Search for the Beloved Community*, p. 101.

³³Martin Luther King, Jr., "A Comparison of the Conceptions of God in the Thinking of Paul Tillich and Henry Nelson Wieman" (Ph.D. dissertation, Boston University, 1955), p. 333.

³⁴*Ibid.*, p. 167.

³⁵*Ibid.*, p. 270.

³⁶*Ibid.*, p. 272.

³⁷*Ibid.*, p. 275.

³⁸*Ibid.*, p. 298.

³⁹King, "How Modern Christians Should Think of Man," essay in the Boston collection.

⁴⁰King, *Strength to Love*, pp. 172-173.

Chapter 2

¹L. D. Reddick, *Crusader Without Violence* (New York: Harper and Row, Publishers, Inc., 1959), pp. 80-81.

²Martin Luther King, Jr., *Stride Toward Freedom: The Montgomery Story* (New York: Harper and Row, Publishers, Inc., 1958), p. 78.

³*Ibid.*, pp. 78, 79.

⁴Louis Lomax, *The Negro Revolt* (New York: Harper and Row, Publishers, Inc.,

1962), p. 81.
⁵King, *Stride Toward Freedom*, p. 29.
⁶Lerone Bennett, *What Manner of Man: A Biography of Martin Luther King, Jr.*, (New York: Pocket Books, 1968), p. 59.
⁷*Ibid.*, pp. 44-45.
⁸Lomax, *The Negro Revolt*, p. 84.
⁹Lionel Lokos, *House Divided: The Life and Legacy of Martin Luther King* (Westport, Conn.: Arlington House Publishers, 1968), p. 90.
¹⁰King, *Stride Toward Freedom*, p. 138.
¹¹*Ibid.*, p. 139.
¹²*Ibid.*, p. 140.
¹³*Ibid.*, p. 66.
¹⁴*Ibid.*, pp. 66-67.
¹⁵Louis Lomax, *To Kill a Black Man* (Los Angeles: Holloway House, 1968), p. 89.
¹⁶Jim Bishop, *The Days of Martin Luther King, Jr.* (New York: G.P. Putnam's Sons, 1971), p. 253.
¹⁷David L. Lewis, *King: A Critical Biography* (New York: Penguin Books, 1970), p. 96.
¹⁸Coretta S. King, *My Life with Martin Luther King, Jr.* (New York: Avon Books, 1970), p. 172.
¹⁹*Ibid.*, pp. 186-187.
²⁰King, *Stride Toward Freedom*, p. 71.
²¹Coretta S. King, *My Life with Martin Luther King, Jr.*, p. 274.
²²Martin Luther King, Jr., *Strength to Love* (New York: Harper and Row, Publishers, Inc., 1963), pp. 169-170.

Chapter 3

¹Lerone Bennett, *What Manner of Man: A Biography of Martin Luther King, Jr.* (New York: Pocket Books, 1968), p. 82.
²Martin Luther King, Jr., *The Trumpet of Conscience* (New York: Harper and Row, Publishers, Inc., 1968), p. 15.
³*Ibid.*, pp. 59, 62.
⁴Howard Zinn, *SNCC: The New Abolitionists* (Boston: Beacon Press, 1965), p. 123.
⁵Alan F. Westin and Barry Mahoney, *The Trial of Martin Luther King, Jr.* (New York: Thomas Y. Crowell Co., 1974), pp. 45-46.
⁶David L. Lewis, *King: A Critical Biography* (New York: Penguin Books, 1970), p. 156.
⁷Martin Luther King, Jr., *Why We Can't Wait* (New York: Harper and Row, Publishers, Inc., 1963), p. 43.
⁸*Ibid.*, p. 44.
⁹Lewis, *King*, p. 192.
¹⁰Westin and Mahoney, *The Trial of Martin Luther King, Jr.*, p. 46.
¹¹King, *Why We Can't Wait*, pp. 70-71.
¹²Bennett, *What Manner of Man*, p. 152.
¹³*Ibid.*, p. 153.
¹⁴King, *Why We Can't Wait*, pp. 105-106.
¹⁵Charles Fager, *Selma 1965: The Town Where the South Was Changed* (New York: Charles Scribner's Sons, 1974), p. 34.
¹⁶George Breitman, ed., *Malcolm X Speaks* (New York: Grove Press, Inc., 1965), p. 9.

[17] Westin and Mahoney, *The Trial of Martin Luther King, Jr.*, pp. 152-153, 165.

[18] King claims that he did not make any commitment to the plan. See his article "Behind the Selma March," *Saturday Review* (April 3, 1965), p. 57. Other authors — such as David Garrow in *Protest at Selma: Martin Luther King, Jr., and the Voting Rights Act of 1965* (New Haven: Yale University Press, 1978), p. 86; Charles Fager in *Selma 1965*, p. 102; William R. Miller in *Martin Luther King, Jr.: His Life, Martyrdom and Meaning for the World* (New York: Weybright and Talley, Inc., 1968), p. 222; and Lewis in *King: A Critical Biography*, p. 279 — feel differently.

[19] Lewis, *King*, p. 294.

[20] Fager, *Selma 1965*, p. 212.

[21] Louis Lomax, *To Kill a Black Man* (Los Angeles: Holloway House, 1968), p. 161.

Chapter 4

[1] Martin Luther King, Jr., *Where Do We Go From Here: Chaos or Community?* (New York: Harper and Row, Publishers, Inc., 1967), p. 5.

[2] "Playboy Interview with Martin Luther King," *Playboy* (January 1965), pp. 70-71. Copyright © 1965 by Playboy.

[3] Lionel Lokos, *House Divided: The Life and Legacy of Martin Luther King* (Westport, Conn.: Arlington House Publishers, 1968), p. 234.

[4] King, *Where Do We Go From Here?* pp. 135-136.

[5] Coretta S. King, *My Life with Martin Luther King, Jr.* (New York: Avon Books, 1970), p. 287.

[6] Martin Luther King, Jr., *The Trumpet of Conscience* (New York: Harper and Row, Publishers, Inc., 1968), p. 14.

[7] David L. Lewis, *King: A Critical Biography* (New York: Penguin Books, 1970), pp. 302-303.

[8] *WNET, Bill Moyers Journal*, April 2, 1979, "Andrew Young Remembers Martin Luther King," p. 12.

[9] Martin Luther King, Jr., "Advice for Living," *Ebony*, vol. 13, no. 11 (September 1958), p. 68.

[10] Martin Luther King, *Stride Toward Freedom* (New York: Harper and Row, Publishers, Inc., 1958), p. 204; and *Why We Can't Wait* (New York: Harper and Row, Publishers, Inc., 1963), p. 152.

[11] Martin Luther King, Jr., *Strength to Love* (New York: Harper and Row, Publishers, Inc., 1963), p. 171.

[12] King, "Dreams of Brighter Tomorrows," *Ebony*, vol. 20, no. 5 (March 1965), p. 34.

[13] Martin Luther King, Jr., "A Time to Break Silence," *Freedomways*, vol. 7, no. 2 (second quarter), 1967, p. 108. Reprinted with permission.

[14] *Ibid.*, pp. 116-117.

[15] Jim Bishop, *The Days of Martin Luther King, Jr.* (New York: G. B. Putnam's Sons, 1971), p. 453.

[16] David Halberstam, "When 'Civil Rights' and 'Peace' Join Forces," in *Martin Luther King: A Profile*, ed. C. Eric Lincoln (New York: Hill and Wang, 1970), pp. 205-206.

[17] Lokos, *House Divided*, p. 404.

[18] Bishop, *The Days of Martin Luther King, Jr.*, p. 428.

[19] Coretta S. King, *My Life with Martin Luther King, Jr.*, p. 297.

[20] John Williams, *The King God Didn't Save: Reflections on the Life and Death of Martin Luther King, Jr.*, (New York: Simon and Schuster, 1971), p. 171.

[21] *Ibid.*, p. 172.

Chapter 5

[1] Martin Luther King, Jr., *Stride Toward Freedom: The Montgomery Story* (New York: Harper and Row, Publishers, Inc., 1958), pp. 83-88.

[2] Harold Cruse, *Rebellion or Revolution* (New York: William Morrow and Company, Inc., 1968), pp. 76-77.

[3] John Oliver Killens, *Black Man's Burden* (New York: Simon and Schuster, 1965), p. 118.

[4] *Ibid.*, p. 116.

[5] Reinhold Niebuhr, *Moral Man and Immoral Society*, (New York: Charles Scribner's Sons, 1932 (1960), p. 252.

[6] King, *Stride Toward Freedom*, p. 80.

[7] *Ibid.*

[8] *Ibid.*, p. 195.

[9] Roger Shinn, *Tangled World* (New York: Charles Scribner's Sons, 1965), pp. 79-80.

[10] Niebuhr, *Moral Man and Immoral Society*, p. 240.

[11] *Ibid.*, p. 241.

[12] Hanes Walton, *The Political Philosophy of Martin Luther King, Jr.*, (Westport, Conn.: Greenwood Publishing Corporation, 1971), pp. 82-83.

[13] Niebuhr, *Moral Man and Immoral Society*, p. 252.

[14] Martin Luther King, Jr., *Where Do We Go from Here: Chaos or Community?* (New York: Harper and Row, Publishers, Inc., 1967), p. 152.

[15] Shinn, *Tangled World*, p. 18.

[16] Herbert Richardson, "Martin Luther King — Unsung Theologian," *New Theology*, no. 6, Martin Marty and Dean Peerman, eds. (New York: Macmillan Inc., 1969), p. 180.

[17] King, *Where Do We Go from Here?*, p. 72.

[18] Niebuhr, *Moral Man and Immoral Society*, p. 249.

[19] *Ibid.*, p. 250.

[20] Walton, *The Political Philosophy of Martin Luther King, Jr.*, p. 80.

[21] John Swomley, Jr., *Liberation Ethics* (New York: Macmillan Inc., 1972), p. 172.

[22] King, *Stride Toward Freedom*, p. 194.

[23] Bennie Goodwin, *Dr. Martin Luther King, Jr: God's Messenger of Love, Justice and Hope* (Jersey City: Goodpatrick Publishers, 1976), p. 33.

[24] Niebuhr, *Moral Man and Immoral Society*, p. 247.

[25] Killens, *Black Man's Burden*, p. 111.

[26] Walton, *The Political Philosophy of Martin Luther King, Jr.*, pp. 83-84.

[27] King, *Strength to Love*, pp. 171-172.

[28] King, *Stride Toward Freedom*, p. 87.

[29] *Ibid.*, p. 88.

[30] Walton, *The Political Philosophy of Martin Luther King, Jr.*, pp. 79-80.

[31] Gene Sharp, *The Politics of Nonviolent Action* (Boston: Porter Sargent Publishers, Inc., 1973), p. 635.

[32] King, *Strength to Love*, p. 46.

[33] King, *Stride Toward Freedom*, p. 88.

[34] *Ibid.*, p. 193.

[35] Coretta S. King, *My Life With Martin Luther King, Jr.*, (New York: Avon Books, 1969), p. 316.

Conclusion

[1] H. H. Gerth and C. Wright Mills, tr.,ed., *From Max Weber: Essays in Sociology*, (New York: Oxford University Press, Inc., 1946), p. 121.

[2] Martin Luther King, Jr., *The Trumpet of Conscience* (New York: Harper and Row, Publishers, Inc., 1968), pp. 76-78.

Index